PUBLIC, MUNICIPAL AND COMMUNITY BUILDINGS

Architectural Record Books

Architectural Record Series Books

PUBLIC, MUNICIPAL AND COMMUNITY BUILDINGS

by Charles King Hoyt, AIA

An Architectural Record Book  McGraw-Hill Book Company

New York
St. Louis
San Francisco
Auckland
Bogotá
Düsseldorf
Johannesburg
London
Madrid
Mexico

Montreal
New Delhi
Panama
Paris
São Paulo
Singapore
Sydney
Tokyo
Toronto

The editors for this book were Jeremy Robinson and
Patricia Markert.
The production supervisors were Elizabeth Dineen and Paul A. Malchow
The book was set in Optima and Helios by Post Graphics
and Jemet, Inc.
Printed and bound by Halliday Lithograph Corporation.

Library of Congress Cataloging in Publication Data

Main entry under title:

Public, municipal, and community buildings.

"An Architectural record book."

Includes index.

1. Public Buildings. 2. Community Centers.

3. Architecture, Modern--20th century. I. Hoyt,

Charles King.

NA4170.P82   725   79-13681

ISBN 0-07-002351-4

CONTENTS

PREFACE

THE GOVERNMENT BUILDS: CITY HALLS TO FIREHOUSES TO PARKS

The recent generation of public buildings and facilities has shown a heightened sense of government's responsibilities—especially in design quality and refinement of function to meet more clearly recognized needs. The first four chapters in this book group the results of construction during this generation into broad categories that—while covering only a sampling of the best examples—clearly illustrate these heightened responsibilities in the built executions. The categories are: buildings and facilities for government's basic functioning (offices, courts and city hall); buildings for public services (firehouses, post offices, police stations and jails); and buildings for parks, recreation and cultural pursuits.

A fifth chapter shows the merits of multi-use facilities, a relatively new but rapidly growing category of construction that responds to both the need for public economies and the increasing complexity of operations. For the purposes of this book, multi-use facilities include civic centers, community centers and the like that may or may not respond to the greatest new advantage of such clusterings, the ability to use the same expensive spaces for more than one purpose. (If in fact there is no such flexibility, the multi-use center which simply groups functions does respond to economics in the ease of interaction that it allows, but above all it is probably responding to a growing fashion for neatly grouping functions in all fields of endeavor.) A stunning example of a flexibly planned civic building is architects' Ciardullo Ehmann's South Paterson Library and Community Center in the fifth chapter, a facility that well might not have been affordable without the economic advantages of combining a number of neighborhood uses under one roof.

As readers pass through the pages of these five chapters, they will undoubtedly be struck by the vast changes in what governments have seen fit to build with public monies since the "bare bones" era that immediately followed the Second World War. (This theme is developed further in the introduction to Chapter One.) And while the reader may immediately envision the spectre of higher taxes to pay for better buildings, the question may once again be raised: just how much does good architecture cost when we are talking about buildings that are going to be expensive even if only the bare bones are built? Often the answer may be only a fraction more, or nothing at all.

Often the success of a building may be more a question of good versus bad concepts—as was the case with architect William Morgan's revolutionary and economical combination of the Jacksonville Police Headquarters with a park shown in Chapter Two. Looked at another way, are buildings really a good buy at any cost when they are uncomfortable to be in, unpleasant to look at—or worst of all—non-functional. And even though there may be strong arguments against building anything as lavish as, say, architects Piano + Roger's Georges Pompidou National Center in Chapter Four, there are certainly moments of civic pride when construction monies so well applied seem worth all the cost—in the spirit of the great nineteenth-century public extravaganzas.

ertainly, this current crop of public buildings is a product of a higher regard for the individuals who must work in them, for the public who must or want to have dealings in them and for the immediate neighborhoods that they occupy. Newly expanded standards for space, lighting, comfort and amenity characterize these structures. And there is a new element in their design that was virtually forgotten in the postwar era: reinforcement of the character of the surrounding neighborhood. (Often government construction, from courthouses to libraries, had been just disastrous for the established characters of downtowns across the country.) It is therefore a pleasure to note a more sympathetic attitude—be it architects Woolen Associates' urban Pilot Center for Cincinnati (Chapter Five) or architects Philip Ives Associates' rural Ann Mason visitors' center (Chapter Four). The latter must accommodate not only the countryside, but an historic adjacent house as well. These are buildings that fit into their contexts and realize one of government's most important—if not always practiced—roles: regard for individuals, who are in this case the neighbors and passersby.

nother new concept of governments' responsibilities to the built environment (and to economies as well) is witnessed by the large number of fine older buildings in this book that are being recycled for public purposes. These range from the spectacular nineteenth-century public library that has been remodeled by architects Holabird & Root into the Chicago Cultural Center to architects' Gunn & Meyerhoff's modest visitors' center for Savannah, (both in Chapter Four). An article by architect Ben Weese in Chapter One on rediscovering county courthouses is designed to whet the appetites of those who would further the recycling cause. This cause is clearly filtering down to local and state governments from the Federal level, which now dictates the re-use of older buildings whenever possible. And this mandatory policy is bound to affect the work of all concerned with any level of government construction—if not because of sympathy with the past, then because of rising construction costs.

he selection of building types in each category has been made as broad as possible. That is, the buildings reflect built responses to sets of circumstances as these circumstances affect size, location and function—despite ostensibly similar labels. For instance, two buildings in Chapter Three are labeled youth recreation centers. One, the Saint Peters Park Recreation Center by architects Ciardullo Ehmann is located in a poor ghetto area of urban Newark, New Jersey—it provides minimal enclosed areas as a reflection of both a very low budget and maintenance and security problems. (Accordingly the building is conceived as a light-hearted pavilion that is the central focus of largely outdoor activities.) On the other hand, architects Ferendino/Grafton/Spillis/Candela's large suburban Miami Beach Youth Center—located in an affluent neighborhood, built with a substantial budget—offers the widest possible range of enclosed facilities, including an ice-skating rink and pinball machines. Similarly, "police stations" in Chapter Two range from architects Gruzen & Partners' massive New York City Police Headquarters to architects Feibes & Schmidt's relatively tiny Schenectady Police Headquarters.

arge or small, low or tall, urban or suburban, Northeastern or Southeastern, Federal or municipal, the buildings on the following pages represent a pleasing survey of what governments have been up to for the last decade or so. Like the great nineteenth-century public monuments, they are fitting sources of public pride—for our generation.

Charles K. Hoyt

CHAPTER ONE

BUILDINGS FOR GOVERNMENTS' BASIC FUNCTIONING: CITY HALLS, COURTHOUSES, OFFICES, AND GOVERNMENT CENTERS

The recent past has spawned the concept of "centers"—be they for shopping, culture, amusement or whatever. And government has not been exempted. It is no coincidence that most of the buildings in which governments carry on day-to-day functions are contained in government centers, as shown in this chapter. These groupings of buildings—while often creating what some think is an unfortunate isolation from the life of downtown streets—do offer opportunities for the special and large scale architectural expression that is often thought appropriate for public functions.

Until after the Second World War, buildings such as city halls and courthouses were imbued with monumental character to express civic aspirations and pride. Large scale, rich ornamentation and lavish materials were the norm. But in the more sober mood that immediately followed the War, such buildings often reflected stripped down efficiency at the expense of amenity. And this trend was certainly in line with the reigning concept of civic responsibility; economy (or the appearance of economy) above most else. Unfortunately the "most else" included not only monumentality (courthouses could now look like supermarkets), but often some very human considerations, like the public's right not to be herded into oppressive environments—when for instance exercising such civic responsibilities as jury duty.

The buildings on the following pages restore stature to the image of government. They are also commodious, efficient, comfortable and pleasant to be in. And while many of the buildings are in centers, they do not exist in a vacuum. Each building or group of buildings has a special character that recognizes its particular region and immediate environment. For example, the first subject in this chapter, architect Eduardo Catalano's Greensboro Center, is appropriately low in height and open as a reflection of a not-densely-urban and temperate location. And the new buildings have a strong monumental character that visually incorporates a handsome neo-classic older courthouse into their composition. By contrast, the second subject is architect Robert Houvener's Thousand Oaks Center, which has a strong, low-lying "space age" image to compliment the California hills against which it stands. And certainly architect Raymond Moriyama's Scarborough Center is a celebration of government. Fortunately, those in the exercise of government can once again be proud of the physical message that these buildings convey.

GREENSBORO GOVERNMENTAL CENTER

Gordon H. Schenck photos

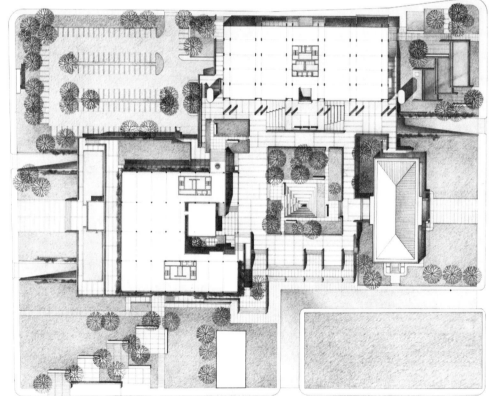

The Governmental Center in Greensboro, North Carolina, is one example of the benefits that can be derived from unified planning policies between city and county governments. Here the city and Guilford County have combined forces to create a complex of buildings in downtown Greensboro on the site of an existing court house (right in the photo opposite). The center is composed of a municipal building (left in the opposite photo and top photo above), a new county court house and office building, the old court house, and a 400-car two-level underground parking garage. The center covers a ten-acre site which slopes about 20 feet, providing the opportunity to open the main levels of the three above-ground buildings to a central plaza, while other levels can be approached directly from the surrounding streets at a lower elevation.

The central plaza has a 90- by 120-foot planter with live oaks, magnolias and junipers; at its center a pyramidal sunken garden leads to a stair and to the parking garage below. The major structural components of the building are precast, with only retaining walls, low parapets, beams and columns cast in place. The structure is lineal in character, with beams and columns on a 24-foot span, and four-foot wide precast double tees with a maximum span of 48 feet. The tees are prestressed in areas with suspended ceilings, but where they are exposed normal reinforcing steel is used.

The municipal building is square in plan, five stories high, and designed for a sixth floor expansion. Below the plaza level there are two floors for the police department, parking for 85 police cars, and general services. The three levels above the plaza are used for administrative and technical offices. An open court (photos above and right) three stories high contains a landscaped area, an exhibition room, and a freestanding council chamber (photo far right). The court was made possible by a provision in the North Carolina building code which allows buildings for office use to have spaces of up to three stories high completely open, as long as the spaces are simply designed, and unobstructed.

The county building is a six-story structure in which the court rooms depart from tradition in the placement of judges and witnesses (photo right); the judge's bench is located at the corner of each room. As a whole the building contains most of the county administration offices on the plaza level, and the second and third floors contain all of the courtroom facilities. The top floor of the building has been built for future expansion.

GOVERNMENTAL CENTER, Greensboro, North Carolina. Architects: *Eduardo Catalano—associate, Peter C. Sugar.* Associate architects: *McMinn, Norfleet & Wicker.* Engineers: *Deborah Forsman* (structural); *Francis Associates* (mechanical/electrical). General contractor: *Weaver Construction Co.*

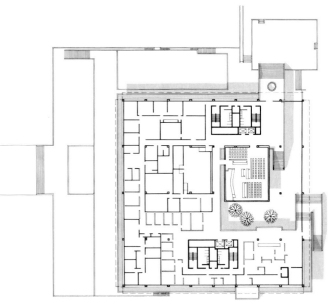

MUNICIPAL BUILDING

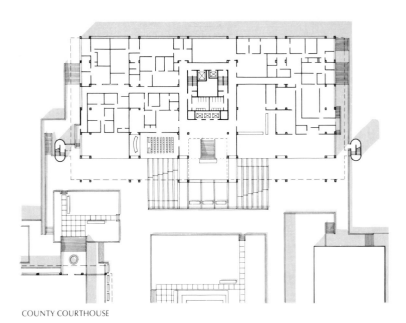

COUNTY COURTHOUSE

Gordon H. Schenck photos

THOUSAND OAKS CIVIC CENTER

Gary Joiner

In April, 1969, the City of Thousand Oaks, California, announced a competition for the design of its new civic center. The site for the new building was a 30-acre parcel of land overlooking the town and adjacent to a major freeway; in spite of its fairly central location, it had an almost rural quality, and was made up of gently rolling hills dotted with oak trees. Architects were invited to submit a masterplan for the entire site, a conceptual design for the ultimate phase of the civic center, and detailed designs for the first two buildings—a city hall and facilities for a chamber of commerce. The challenge of the competition was to make something on a difficult site (and within a fairly tight budget) that would be identifiable as a structure of civic importance, and that would also be in concert with its environment—not just with the physical surroundings, but with the spirit of this growing southern California town.

By September of 1969, 155 architects had responded to the invitation (a response that represented $1.5 million worth of labor, according to one estimate), and their boards were presented to the jury, which included Charles Moore, then dean of the Yale Architecture School, and Cesar Pelli, then a partner of Victor Gruen Associates. The winner was a newcomer, Robert Mason Houvener, who was at the time a project design engineer for the Navy. His building is shown above.

8

In their general comments the jury for the Thousand Oaks Civic Center competition pointed out that while many of the entries were fine, many more were without concept, a lack that was "camouflaged by highly complex and often, in detail, quite pleasant solutions." They went on to conclude that such entries "managed to miss the point of the simplicity and clarity that this building needed in order to work and in order to perform its symbolic function. That is what made the First Prize get the First Prize—sticking to a very simple and strong idea."

Robert Mason Houvener's winning scheme is indeed very simple, a range of one-story buildings in a broad arc high on the hill-side. From the freeway below it is seen as a long white band curving across the land (photo on previous page); parking is on the roof of the buildings and on grade on the uphill side. Inside the buildings (plan left) individual offices tend to face the view, while larger interior spaces open onto landscaped courtyards with stairways leading up to the on-grade parking. It is hard to imagine a more direct approach to the problem. The buildings make a clear image for themselves as they accommodate the required functions inside. They make it clear how you arrive and how you enter. They show that this is a public place, but one which nevertheless respects the natural site. They look like they ought to be there.

Gary Joiner

J. Spencer Lake

Buildings designed around a strong, simple and consistent concept are often unsatisfactory in some of their details—where what seems ideal in one particular part may not fit the format of the whole. In the case of the Thousand Oaks Civic Center what is required to make the bold image shown on the previous pages is not automatically suited, for instance, to the desirable scale for pedestrians who, after they have parked their cars, approach and enter. But the architect has gone to considerable effort here to soften the feeling of the uphill side of the building without actually changing its over-all concept. The plan and photograph on the previous two pages show how, on this side, the continuous sweep of the façade is broken up into a series of small outdoor spaces by the bridges that lead from the approach road to the roof parking. These spaces are populated by stairs, ramps, small trees and plants that make this side of the building as inviting as the other side is imposing. The photographs above show one of these spaces from three different vantages; it is the entrance to the council chamber used for ceremony.

THOUSAND OAKS CIVIC CENTER, Thousand Oaks, California. Architect: *Robert Mason Houvener.* Engineers: *A. J. Blaylock & Associates* (structural, mechanical and electrical); *Moore & Taber* (foundations). Consultants: *James Dean & Associates* (landscape); *Albert R. Vallin* (cost). General contractor: *Ralph T. Viola Co.*

James Wheat

Gary Joiner

Hennepin County Government Center

An important new public building has been designed as the focal point of a developing civic center in Minneapolis. In a bold design approach, John Carl Warnecke & Associates provided a public space in the grand tradition of civic buildings that is also compatible with today's needs, a scheme that combines what the architects refer to as "informality within monumentality."

Philip MacMillan James photos except as noted

Completion of the Hennepin County Government Center in Minneapolis marks the beginning of a new civic center that will encompass an 18-block area when completed. The civic center's master plan (also designed by the Warnecke firm) was premised on the design of this building as the focal point of the area. While the plan establishes guidelines for future public and private development within the parameters (including the location, height and bulk of buildings, and the position of open spaces—all interconnected by pedestrian aerial walkways), it does so with all aspects relating to the Center.

The Center's design concept was based on an exemplary planning process by both the architects and a facilities analysis and design firm, SUA, Inc. SUA began an extensive, detailed space utilization study in 1965; its recommendations subsequently stimulated the passage of 23 bills by the state legislature that reorganized the county government. One major recommendation which affected the design was the separation of county administration offices from the district and municipal courts. To express these two distinct services, a 24-story twin-tower design evolved (the east tower housing judicial facilities, the west tower housing offices).

The outstanding feature of the building, however, is a 350-foot-high atrium created between the towers, bordered dramatically with exposed steel diagonal bracing. It is a great indoor space, enjoyed by the public and the employees—fully appreciated as a controlled, year-round environment, not affected by the changeability and severity of the Midwest's weather. The atrium is flooded with light through a combination of glass end walls and a large skylight. At the roof line, enormous exposed steel tetrahedrons frame this skylight and the corridors of the top floor.

By siting the structure so the inner court aligns with the towers of the old Municipal Building across the street (designed by Long and Kees on 1906) and by using glass curtain walls on this axis, views from the atrium are opened up and primarily focused on the old building, signifying the relationship and continued coordination of services between the two structures. Compatibility of the two buildings is further enhanced by the use of red granite on the new building's facade complementing the older facade.

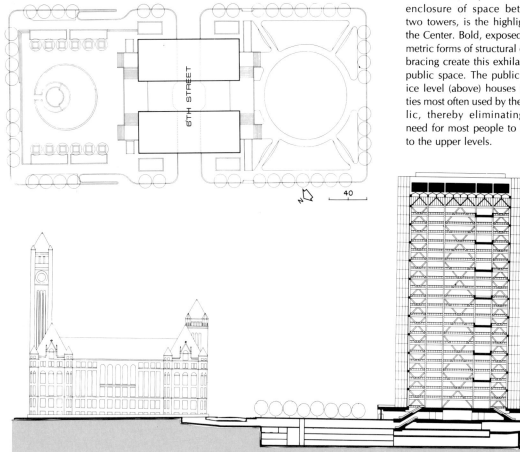

An interior court, formed by the enclosure of space between two towers, is the highlight of the Center. Bold, exposed geometric forms of structural cross-bracing create this exhilarating public space. The public service level (above) houses facilities most often used by the public, thereby eliminating the need for most people to travel to the upper levels.

A unique structural system solved the inherent engineering problems of the atrium concept. Diagonal wind-bracing was positioned on the interior walls facing the atrium rather than on the perimeter of the building, and exposed the full height of the court. The total space frame acts like a cage, stiffening the building's frame, minimizing building drift and allowing 85 per cent usable floor space in the towers. It accepts lateral loads (transmitted from the composite floors through diaphragm action) and distributes the stresses downward throughout the 180-foot building length. The cage is supported below the public service level by 30-inch thick concrete shear walls, constructed on bedrock. The building spans a street using a conventional support system (rolled structural steel shapes, designed compositely, with a concrete topping slab).

Because the Center spans a street, spaces were created for two large landscaped parks. Recycled water from the north plaza fountain flows one story below the street level, and can be seen from a large cafeteria. This level also connects the two government buildings and houses jury, computer, mail and printing facilities.

In 1976, a total cost of $49.3 million for the building (not including $1.9 million for landscaping and site work) was achieved. This is a surprisingly low $34 per square foot, with a large part of the savings resulting from the structural ingenuity of the diagonal bracing, which required less steel and fewer complicated connections of members than in many more conventional systems.

Roberts Associates, Minneapolis

HENNEPIN COUNTY GOVERNMENT CENTER, Minneapolis, Minnesota. Architects; *John Carl Warnecke & Associates: Peterson, Clarke and Associates, Inc.* (associates). Engineers: *Ketchum, Konkel, Barrett, Nickel and Austin* (structural); *Jacus and Amble* (associate structural); *Donald Bentley and Associates* (mechanical/electrical/plumbing); *Michaud, Cooley, Hallberg, Erickson & Associates* (associate mechanical/electrical/plumbing). Consultant: *SUA Incorporated* (facilities analysis/planning/design). Interior design: *SUA Incorporated.* Landscape architect: *Michael Painter & Associates.* Construction management: *Construction Management Services, Inc.* General contractor: *Knutson Construction Company.*

Leo Holub

Despite a noticeable difference between the interior tower facades bordering the court (only one side is glazed for acoustical reasons) there is no air conditioning imbalance throughout the 4.3 million cubic foot court space, for a wall set back beyond a corridor in the opposite tower performs an offsetting effect. Seven elevated walkways (spaced every third floor above the public service level) span the court, connecting the two towers. Eventually a series of elevated bridges will connect this building with others in the civic center.

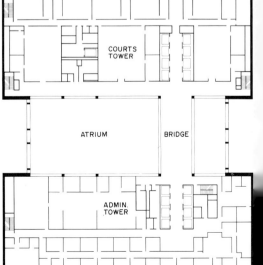

Bruce Barnbaum

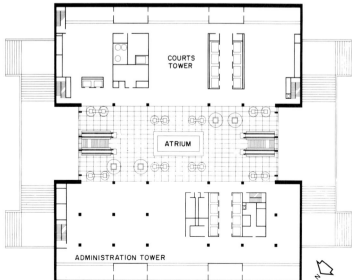

PUBLIC SERVICE LEVEL

TYPICAL LEVEL

Santa Cruz County Governmental Center

In these two buildings for
Santa Cruz County, California,
the unusual architectural statement results in
a lively and highly articulated exterior
whose directness and honesty is further
expressed in the interior. There, mechanical
and electrical systems are treated as elements
in the design and are forthrightly left
exposed throughout virtually the
entire complex. What might have been an
uncompromising principle of ruggedness is turned,
by precise and elegant detail,
into a clear statement of strong conviction.
Precast and prestressed elements
are used repetitively to achieve
an unusual degree of economy.

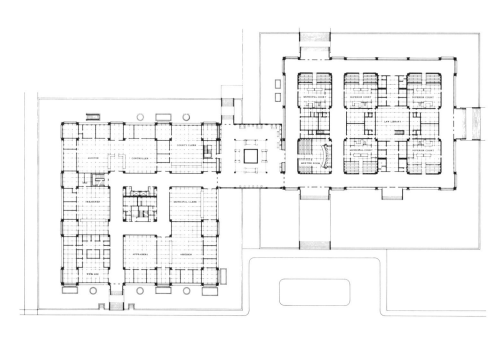

GROUND FLOOR PLAN

The site is a 10.3-acre plot
beside a river which meanders
through the city of Santa Cruz.
The openness of the site
gives the new complex
exceptional prominence in
the community, a town destined
to grow with the development
of the University of California's
new campus in the hill above town.
The architects had design control
of site details such as
lighting in parking areas.
The bridge between office
and courthouse buildings (below, right)
forms a sheltered open-air courtyard
with benches and potted shrubs.

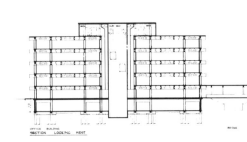

OFFICE
BUILDING
SECTION LOOKING WEST   BRIDGE   COURT HOUSE

The county governmental center in Santa Cruz, California, consists of two buildings: the five-story administrative office building and a one-story courthouse, linked by a glass-walled bridge open to the sky. The center stands free of other buildings in a redevelopment area along the San Lorenzo river. The highly articulated exterior of the office building, and the dignified courthouse, rely on precast concrete elements, used repetitively and with great sucess, to achieve union of design scheme and structure. The interiors of both buildings deal with mechanical and electrical systems on their own terms, but treat them openly as elements of the design. These unusual and individual buildings are at once elegant in the precision of their detail and rugged in their over-all appearance. They achieve exceptional flexibility in the use of space through long clear spans and the elimination of suspended ceilings, and are economical in cost. The unusual structural system uses 17.5-foot-square towers of poured-in-place concrete, set 55 feet on center, and exposed Vierendeel trusses (some prestressed, some conventionally reinforced) which carry the mechanical and electrical systems. A five foot module, respected throughout, permitted extensive repetitive procedures.

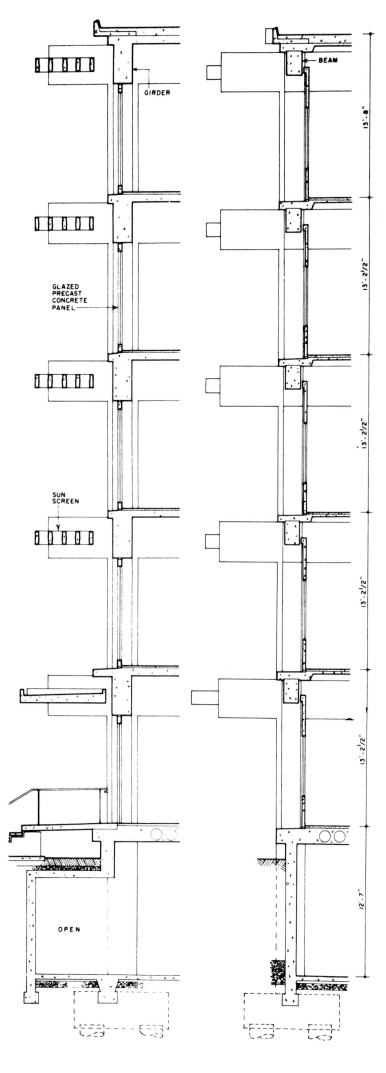

GIRDER

BEAM

GLAZED
PRECAST
CONCRETE
PANEL

SUN
SCREEN

13'-8"

13'-2½"

13'-2½"

13'-2½"

13'-2½"

12'-7"

OPEN

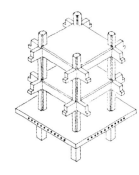

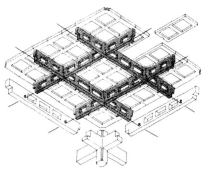

The four cruciform columns
that make up each tower
are tied together by girders whose
cantilevered brackets are
designed to support the Vierendeel
trusses that are widely used
in both buildings to carry the
precast concrete panels of the
floor slab. The stub ends
of girders project beyond the face
of the building in an unusual
architectural expression of
the structural system, and carry
sunscreens to shield the large
corner offices and conference rooms.
Suspended light fixtures (below)
define the ceiling line
in public offices (left)
and conference rooms (right).

Dignified and handsome, the courthouse uses the same structural concept, varied to permit the courtroom arrangement. Its exterior is a window wall of precast concrete elements, repeated on all four sides. It is the interior, however, that tells the story of the building. The courtrooms are surrounded by a spacious gallery which acts as public lobby as well as circulation. This pleasant space, broad and high, is daylighted by the windows on the building's periphery. The courtrooms, in contrast, have no windows but are daylighted from above by an ingenious and subtle means: skylights, set in a pattern that follows the wall line of the courtrooms, transmit light to the corridors which reaches the court-rooms through glass filler panels in the Vierendeel trusses. The quality of the light so diffused is exceptional, both for general use and for reading. On dark days and at night, indirect lighting comes from simple and straightforward light fixtures suspended in a square pattern.

SANTA CRUZ COUNTY GOVERNMENTAL CENTER, Santa Cruz, California. Architects: *Rockwell and Banwell—Charles Hanf, project architect, Charles Holcomb, field supervision;* structural engineers: *Nicholas Forell & Associates;* mechanical engineers: *Kasin, Guttman & Associates;* electrical engineers: *Smith & Garthorne;* acoustical engineer: *Dariel Fitzroy;* landscape architects: *Royston, Hanamoto, Beck & Abby;* contractor: *Jasper Contruction.*

Daylighting of the courthouse
is unusual and exceptionally
pleasant: corridors
receive direct light from
skylights (as well as
from peripheral windows)
that surround each
courtroom. Courtrooms are
daylighted from the same source,
but indirectly, since
light is transmitted to them
through glazed openings
in the Vierendeel trusses
above the courtroom walls.

A CIVIC CENTER FOR SCARBOROUGH, ONTARIO— DESIGNED BY RAYMOND MORIYAMA TO CELEBRATE THE DRAMA OF LOCAL GOVERNMENT AT WORK

These days, an architect who creates a monument gets accused of taking an ego trip, and the monument—say his critics—is to himself. Monumental architecture built today is condemned with passion by almost everyone who speaks or writes about architecture. It has been almost forgotten that such architecture, while usually inappropriate, still has its place—especially in buildings where the arts of government are practiced. For democracy to function, people must understand how it works and a good way for them to learn is at the local level from a building which by its form instructs. A building which clarifies, interprets and dramatizes the administration of democratic government while ceremoniously receiving the public, cannot be fitted into one of the standard, anonymous contemporary office building envelopes. If it is successful, it will assume a distinctive form which signals its uniqueness. It will appeal to the mind and emotions as good monuments have always done.

The Scarborough Civic Center by Raymond Moriyama effectively and handsomely celebrates the drama and process of local government and is in itself a memorable image and the hub of the developing town center. As a design, it builds up to a climax reached as one enters its astonishing interior. Any uneasiness which its unorthodox, vaguely Wrightian exterior forms may engender as one approaches, is swept away by the first perception of this powerful space.

All photographs by Robert E. Fischer except as noted

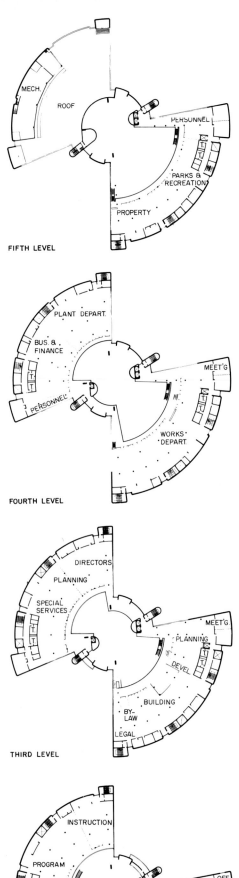

FIFTH LEVEL

MECH. ROOF

PERSONNEL

PARKS & RECREATION

PROPERTY

FOURTH LEVEL

PLANT DEPART.

BUS. & FINANCE

PERSONNEL

MEET'G

WORKS DEPART.

THIRD LEVEL

DIRECTORS

PLANNING

SPECIAL SERVICES

MEET'G

PLANNING

DEVEL

BUILDING

BY-LAW

LEGAL

Scarborough, a part of metropolitan Toronto, is a political entity in its own right with its own borough offices, board of education and board of health, all of which the new civic center accommodates. In designing the project, the firm of Raymond Moriyama, Architects and Planners addressed themselves to a problem of which all the concerned parties were aware—namely that Scarborough, a low-density residential community of single-family houses, had no real center. The total project, therefore, has been designed to give Scarborough a central complex which will be the symbolic heart of the town and the focus for its future.

The building features a splendid multi-storied central space through which the public can move freely. The surrounding floors of open plan offices overlook the public area and together form one continuous space which orients the visitor and makes the building comprehensible to him.

The Scarborough Civic Center is part of a 170-acre development known as Scarborough Town Center which is being master planned by the Toronto firm of Bregman & Hamann and developed by Trizec Equities Ltd. The Town Center is primarily commercial and already boasts a 130-store, Y-shaped shopping center, also planned by Bregman & Hamann and in the future will include office buildings, a hotel and high-rise apartments. The area had originally been zoned industrial by the Scarborough council. The developers got their zoning change by coming up with a scheme for a shopping center and town square with a civic building as its focus, donating the land which had been selected for the construction of the borough facilities. This unusual trade-off was largely the work of the late former

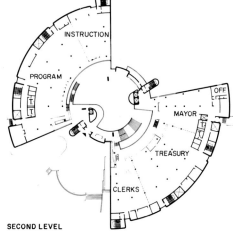

SECOND LEVEL

INSTRUCTION

PROGRAM

OFF

MAYOR

TREASURY

CLERKS

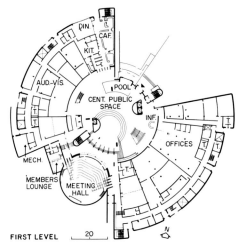

FIRST LEVEL   20   N

DIN.

CAF

KIT

AUD-VIS.

POOL

CENT. PUBLIC SPACE

INF.

OFFICES

MECH.

MEMBERS LOUNGE

MEETING HALL

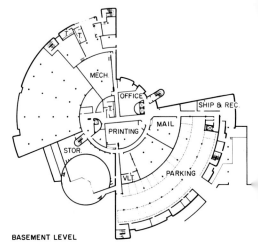

BASEMENT LEVEL

MECH.

OFFICE

SHIP & REC

PRINTING

MAIL

STOR.

VLT

PARKING

A CIVIC CENTER FOR SCARBOROUGH, ONTARIO— DESIGNED BY RAYMOND MORIYAMA TO CELEBRATE THE DRAMA OF LOCAL GOVERNMENT AT WORK

These days, an architect who creates a monument gets accused of taking an ego trip, and the monument—say his critics—is to himself. Monumental architecture built today is condemned with passion by almost everyone who speaks or writes about architecture. It has been almost forgotten that such architecture, while usually inappropriate, still has its place—especially in buildings where the arts of government are practiced. For democracy to function, people must understand how it works and a good way for them to learn is at the local level from a building which by its form instructs. A building which clarifies, interprets and dramatizes the administration of democratic government while ceremoniously receiving the public, cannot be fitted into one of the standard, anonymous contemporary office building envelopes. If it is successful, it will assume a distinctive form which signals its uniqueness. It will appeal to the mind and emotions as good monuments have always done.

The Scarborough Civic Center by Raymond Moriyama effectively and handsomely celebrates the drama and process of local government and is in itself a memorable image and the hub of the developing town center. As a design, it builds up to a climax reached as one enters its astonishing interior. Any uneasiness which its unorthodox, vaguely Wrightian exterior forms may engender as one approaches, is swept away by the first perception of this powerful space.

All photographs by Robert E. Fischer except as noted

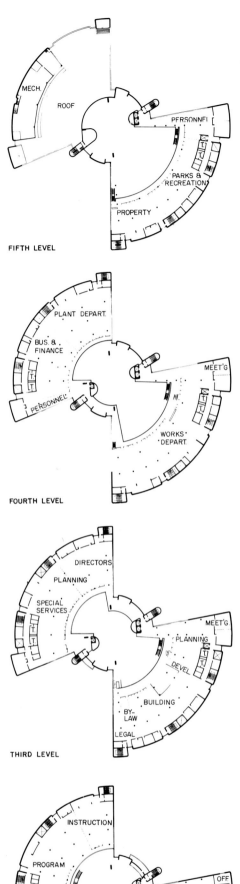

FIFTH LEVEL

FOURTH LEVEL

THIRD LEVEL

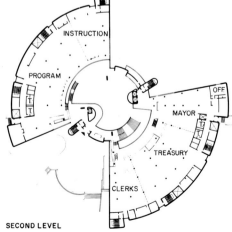

SECOND LEVEL

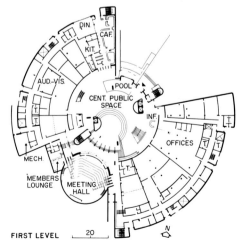

FIRST LEVEL   20   N

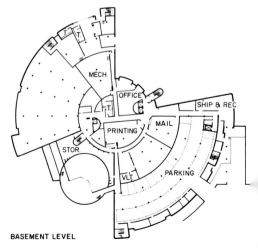

BASEMENT LEVEL

Scarborough, a part of metropolitan Toronto, is a political entity in its own right with its own borough offices, board of education and board of health, all of which the new civic center accommodates. In designing the project, the firm of Raymond Moriyama, Architects and Planners addressed themselves to a problem of which all the concerned parties were aware—namely that Scarborough, a low-density residential community of single-family houses, had no real center. The total project, therefore, has been designed to give Scarborough a central complex which will be the symbolic heart of the town and the focus for its future.

The building features a splendid multi-storied central space through which the public can move freely. The surrounding floors of open plan offices overlook the public area and together form one continuous space which orients the visitor and makes the building comprehensible to him.

The Scarborough Civic Center is part of a 170-acre development known as Scarborough Town Center which is being master planned by the Toronto firm of Bregman & Hamann and developed by Trizec Equities Ltd. The Town Center is primarily commercial and already boasts a 130-store, Y-shaped shopping center, also planned by Bregman & Hamann and in the future will include office buildings, a hotel and high-rise apartments. The area had originally been zoned industrial by the Scarborough council. The developers got their zoning change by coming up with a scheme for a shopping center and town square with a civic building as its focus, donating the land which had been selected for the construction of the borough facilities. This unusual trade-off was largely the work of the late former

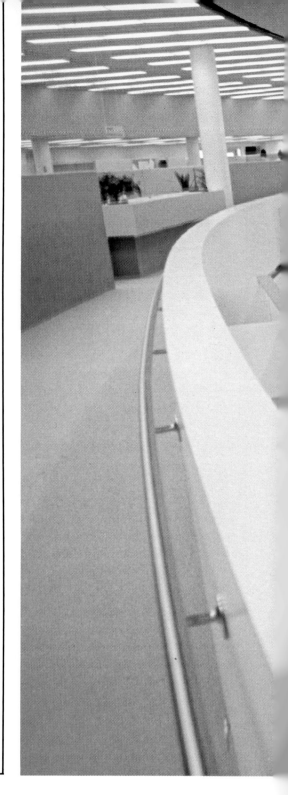

The open plan floors of the borough municipal offices step back. Functions requiring more privacy are located toward the rear of each floor.

Mayor Albert Campbell, after whom the town square has been named.

Moriyama and his firm entered the picture in 1969 with a feasibility study requested by the borough and the board of education to advise them of their land requirements within the Town Center. At this stage, they established the basic design criteria for the civic complex which they were to stick to after receiving the commission to design it. In Moriyama's words, they saw the new center as an opportunity to support and express positive trends such as the demand for openness and accessibility, the desire of the borough residents for a symbol of their collective identity and a need for a focus to draw the attention of outsiders and tourists. From the very first, they affirmed the importance of the proposed town square as a pedestrian domain and as a linchpin for future development in the Town Center.

From the start, Moriyama's firm recommended open planning for the office space in the belief that this approach improves face-to-face communication, relationships between the staff and the public and attracts a high caliber staff. Moriyama's own office has no enclosed private work spaces. Although small, it has a great sense of spaciousness. For Moriyama an open plan building is a democratic building, one in which the public feels it belongs.

The architects' feasibility study advised that the borough and the board of education should cooperate in the planning and financing of certain shared facilities in order to realize savings in capital costs, furnishings, operational and maintenance costs. The municipal offices for the borough and the board of education facilities were to be constructed simultaneously in order to achieve construction and overhead

The entire building is constructed of poured-in-place concrete except for the roof over the central space. It is framed by an 88-foot-diameter ring girder from which radiate 80-foot trusses spanning the office area. The interior walls, ceiling and floor parapets are white and are considerably enlivened by the flags. These were designed by artist James Sutherland to symbolize the functions of the various administrative departments on each level. He also designed the aluminum tetrahedrons (overleaf) and the supergraphics used elsewhere in the building. This central space is joyous and gay, an antidote to bureaucratic fatigue and boredom.

Lee English Biel

This secondary entrance is on the opposite side of the building to the main entrance which faces the town square. It leads to the second level of the structure above the meeting hall.

Lee English Biel

economies. It recommended that the board of health should be part of a linear expansion system, compatible with the main complex but separate because of special financing arrangements.

After receiving the commission to design the building, the architects studied a number of basic forms. Their obvious first option was to design two buildings—one for the board of education and the other for the borough municipal offices. Said Moriyama: "This would have been the easy way out, but it would have made it impossible to meet our larger objectives. We then explored at some length a single building concept allowing free public access through and under the building to the town square. Our conclusion was that a horizontal building would inevitably look like a lobby to the future taller commercial buildings to rise beyond. The physical volume required by the civic center building was not great enough to make a significant tower. Our new building would have to be distinguished by its form, not its size."

The architects began with a split pyramid concept, but after much study turned the half pyramids around so as to face each other across a single public central space. Still dissatisfied and after studying six different variations, they resolved the problem by adopting a flat roof over the central space and using reflective glass in a triangular form on the four elevations.

Another major problem for analysis was the geometry of the layout. The intent was to ensure that the total departmental area requirement could be accommodated in a stepped arrangement based upon a relatively simple structural system. After much study, the architects agreed upon a scheme which radiates from a single center point with two ele-

The town square (left and below) has been designed as a link between the civic building and the mammoth shopping center (not shown). As such, it represents the collaborative efforts of the Moriyama firm and Bregman and Hamann, master planners for the entire Town Center and designers of the shopping center. It has a reflecting pool (below) which in the winter becomes a skating rink. The health building (above) was designed as a separate appendage to the main building because of special financing arrangements. Both the civic and health buildings are sheathed in aluminum siding with a white silicon modified polyester finish. The stainless steel column has circular apertures for lighting and sound facilities. Films can be projected on the walls of the structure.

vator cores and two columns providing the structural basis for a central space 80 feet in diameter and 67 feet high. The floors on the borough side step back on a regular structural bay of 15 feet, while on the board side the floors cantilever out at variable amounts of 6, 11, and 16 feet from a structural column line.

This combination of form and geometry provided the necessary area and flexibility, reinforced the concept of unity, provided a more generous public space at a lower total building volume and allowed visual continuity from one side of the building to the other at all floor levels. Also this geometry and structural system made it possible to interconnect the board of education and the borough municipal offices by means of mezzanines and bridges.

The joint meeting hall (not shown) has been located under the entrance podium and is directly accessible from the central space.

Of special interest is the exterior skin of the building. The basic structure is of poured-in-place concrete including the columns, walls and floor slabs. Thermal insulation has been placed on the exterior of the concrete walls and this has been covered with aluminum siding with a silicon modified polyester finish. This veneer is lightweight, shiny, white and an effective rain screen.

SCARBOROUGH CIVIC CENTER, Scarborough, Ontario. Owners: *Corporation of the Borough of Scarborough, the Board of Education and the Board of Health.* Architects: *Raymond Moriyama, Architects and Planners—James Wilkinson and Ted Tashima associates-in-charge.* Consultants: *Robert Halsall and Associates Ltd.* (structural); *G. Granek and Associates* (mechanical); *Jack Chisvin and Associates Ltd.* (electrical); *James Sutherland* (architectural graphics/sculpture). Construction management: *McDougall Construction Management Ltd.*

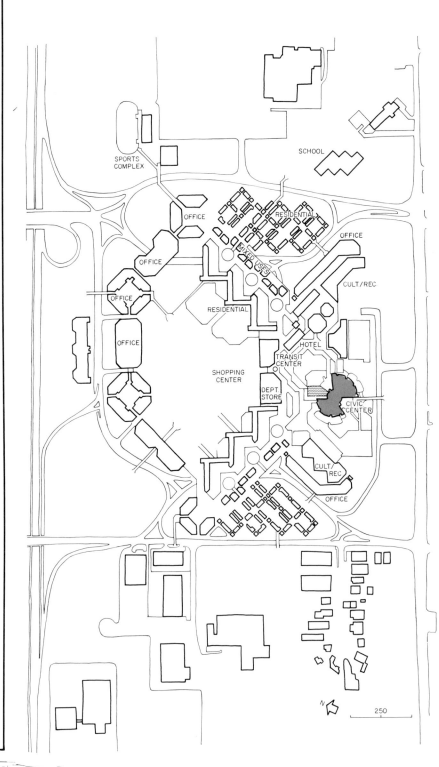

Moriyama has made land use and urban design recommendations for the rest of the 170-acre site.

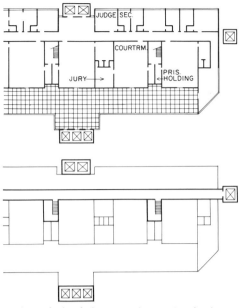

Horizontal circulation (see above). On the lower level are corridors for the public and for the court staff, each with its own elevators. Courtrooms and jury rooms are between the corridors, judges' chambers across the private one. Prisoners are brought in by a third corridor on the upper level.

Vertical circulation (below). Small private lobbies serving pairs of courtrooms are reached by elevators for court staff and for prisoners.

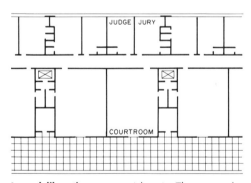

Jury deliberation rooms (above). These can be placed on the outside wall of the building when a horizontal circulation system is used—if there is no objection to the jury walking across the private corridor to reach them.

Future expansion (below). Two diagrams show the schematic possibilities for adding onto a courthouse building without disrupting its operations.

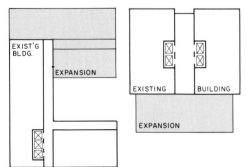

Introductory guidelines for planning a modern courthouse

by Allan Greenberg

The physical organization of the modern courthouse has been completely transformed by the enlarged scale of its operations and the growth of its administrative staff. The problem is not simply one of providing additional courtrooms and office space to cope with an increased case load; it is that the original architectural and functional arrangement of most older courthouses cannot support the court as it now functions, and becomes a hindrance to efficient operations, security and public safety. What is required is a new set of planning guidelines on which the design of new courthouses can be based.

Administrative and judicial functions require very different kinds of space

The first guideline provides for the separation of the administrative and social-service departments from the courtrooms and their associated functions. The latter include judges' chambers, hearing rooms, jury assembly and deliberation rooms, conference rooms and law library. The court's administrative and social-service departments require flexible office space in which the layout of partitions can be altered to respond to administrative or procedural changes. The courtrooms and their associated spaces, on the other hand, are unlikely to change during the life span of the building.

The architectural and engineering characteristics of flexible and permanent space are, of course, quite different, suggesting their separation onto different floors in a multi-story building, or into zones in a one-story courthouse. Normal office partitioning cannot be used for court functions because it is difficult to obtain acoustical privacy. Where acoustical privacy is required, special precautions must be taken which tend to eliminate flexibility. The walls must penetrate the suspended ceiling and be sealed against the structural slab. Pipes and ducts are specially insulated, and the movement of air must be planned to inhibit the transfer of sound. This means that the air-conditioning system has to be tailored to suit a particular layout of rooms, and a change in partition layout requires revamping the whole system. Since permanent spaces serve for the life of the building and since changes are difficult and costly, the information given to the architect about these spaces must be comprehensive and minutely detailed.

Multiple circulation systems are needed in courthouses

Separate systems of corridors, lobbies and elevators must provide access to the courtrooms for the public, for prisoners and for judges, jurors and staff. In most courthouses built be-

----

Allan Greenberg has been Architectural Consultant to the Judicial Department of the State of Connecticut.

fore 1950, public spaces are used by judges, jurors, attorneys, staff and sometimes even prisoners to reach the courtrooms or judges' chambers. Today, considerations of convenience, efficiency and security require that segregated circulation areas be provided.

The horizontal system provides lobbies and corridors to connect *all* the courtrooms on each floor with public, staff, juror and prisoner elevators (see diagram at the left). The public has its own bank of elevators and its own lobby. A private corridor at the rear of the courtrooms is used by judges, staff, and jurors for access to judges' chambers, offices, courtrooms and, if necessary, voir dire (preliminary questioning) rooms. The connections between the private corridor and public lobby must be monitored by a receptionist in order to control access and maintain security. Prisoners use a special corridor, located on a mezzanine level directly above the private corridor, to reach the courtrooms. A staircase connects this corridor to a prisoner holding room adjacent to each courtroom, and a special prison elevator provides vertical circulation from the cell block to the courtroom floors.

The vertical circulation system provides two separate private elevators to serve a series of courtrooms stacked one above the other. One elevator is used to transport prisoners from the cell block to a prisoner holding room adjacent to the courtroom. The other is for the use of judges, jurors and staff. It opens into a private lobby which provides access to the judge's chamber, the rear of the courtroom and, if necessary, a voir dire room. A connection to the public lobby is available for attorneys and members of the public who have appointments to see a judge.

The resulting pattern is of pairs of courtrooms, stacked one above the other on successive floors of the building, grouped around a private staff elevator and lobby. This arrangement has a formative impact on the planning of the rest of the building, since the space on any non-courtroom floor will be interrupted by these private elevators. In the jury assembly room, they must be clearly marked in order to avoid jurors arriving at the wrong courtroom.

The vertical system is best suited to judicial systems in which judges travel on circuit. In this case, a set of resident chambers must be provided for the judges who live in the judicial district. This is in addition to those behind each courtroom for the use of the sitting judges, most of whom will travel to the courthouse from another judicial district. The resident judges' chambers are best located away from the courtrooms, on another floor of the building, preferably near the law library.

The vertical system provides good access between the courtroom floors, the law library, the pool of judges' secretaries, and the various departments of the court. The judges' secretaries serve both sitting and resident judges, but are best located near the resident judges' chambers away from the busy courtrooms. Each department must be planned in proximity to the private elevator core serving the court-

Gerald Allen

Joseph Molitor

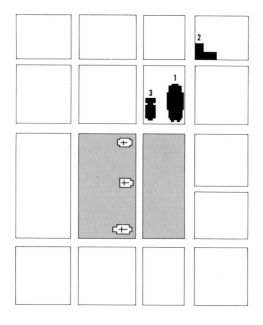

Musical chairs on the New Haven Green

In 1965 the Connecticut Judicial Department was faced with the problem of obsolete facilities and a major shortage of courtrooms and office space in New Haven. The three courts, the higher and lower trial courts and juvenile court, were located, in the City Hall Annex, the Old county courthouse (1), and a late nineteenth century A three-phase solution was developed by the State Judicial Department and Public Works Department. The *first phase* was to plan and construct a new 165,000 square foot building (photo opposite) for the higher trial court on a site (2) across the street from the Old County Courthouse. *Phase two* was to move the lower trial court out of the City Hall Annex into the Old County Courthouse. This robust building of 1913, by William Allen and Richard Williams, is based on the design of St. Georges Hall, Liverpool, by Harvey Lonsdale Elmes. A major renovation of the building was planned. The *third phase* of the plan called for the acquisition of the New Haven library building (3) by the state, and its conversion into a juvenile courthouse. A study indicatied that the building, and excellent Cass Gilbert structure of 1908, could be adapted to the needs of the Juvenile Court with only minor modifification to its splendid interior spaces. This phase of the plan waited for completion of the new city library which is part of a government center complex, designed by Paul Rudolph. This game of musical chairs has resulted in the preservation of two important buildings on this historic New Haven Green, and also saved the taxpayers some hard-earned dollars.

rooms which are used to hear its cases so as to provide for the convenient movement of personnel and documents.

The horizontal system is appropriate when judges are assigned their own courtrooms on a permanent basis. Its main drawback is that jury deliberation rooms are interior, windowless spaces. If there is no objection to the jury walking out of the courtroom, across the private corridor, to jury deliberation rooms on the exterior side of the building, this problem can be circumvented. (See diagram.)

The height of the building is also an important factor in choosing between the horizontal or vertical circulation system. Because of the cost of extra elevators, the vertical circulation system is not suitable to a building of less than six floors.

The circulation system is an important factor in selecting appropriate locations for the various functions and departments in the building. The optimum location depends on interdepartmental communications, public convenience and security, as well as on factors like the volume of visitors and the frequency and nature of the transactions that take place. All this information must be systematically recorded and classified on the basis of priority. One of the most important considerations is that circulation routes in the courthouse should be self-evident.

Architects and court administrators often overlook the fact that the majority of people, especially jurors and witnesses, are in the building for the first time. In many new courthouses, the public experiences considerable difficulty locating both the people and the services they need. When members of the public constantly stop to ask for directions it is a sure sign of a poorly planned building. The majority of visitors usually have destinations in administrative or social service departments. If these are all concentrated on the lower floors of the building, public access is considerably simplified. Some departments may even want a separate entrance directly off the sidewalk.

Centralization has the additional advantage of limiting traffic on courtroom floors to people directly concerned with court proceedings, thereby improving security. The courtrooms should occupy the midsection of the building. The library, judges' chambers, jury assembly room and other areas which require some privacy can be assigned the upper floors. This arrangement results in a division of the building into three zones—office areas, courtrooms and private areas.

Interdepartmental proximity requirements are also an important factor in selecting locations for the various departments and functions. Certain departments require direct access to the private circulation system serving the courtroom for the movement of both court records and personnel. These include the offices of the clerk and the prosecuting attorney, and other departments depending on local circumstances. The segregation of jurors from the public is necessary for efficient control over their movements and to preclude any contact with plaintiffs, defendants, their friends, witnesses, attorneys or other interested parties. For obvious reasons, the connections between the segregated circulation routes and public lobbies must be minimized and carefully controlled. In addition to these "process" factors, the shape and size of the site, the character of the surrounding environment and the zoning restrictions can impose severe limitations on the building's shape, height and floor area, restricting the number of options available for locating departments.

Ways to provide for future expansion in new courthouses

Although future developments are not always predictable, many changes in the court can be anticipated with sufficient certainty to warrant provisions being made to accommodate them in the new building. These may include the creation of new departments, the merging of older ones or, at a smaller scale, the adoption of microfilm for storing records. The initial phase of expansion (10-15 years) is best included in the new building. A difficult question to resolve is whether to provide this space on one or two floors that remain unused until needed, or to distribute it in smaller units on each floor of the building. In the office areas, it is advisable to provide an additional safeguard by making generous initial space allocations. The movable partitions can be rearranged to accommmodate additional personnel and equipment as the work load increases. Provision for eventual expansion by new building also requires careful thought. The circulation system and elevator locations must be planned at the beginning in order to achieve a good and economical connection to a future addition to the courthouse.

Public convenience should be a major design consideration

The public is composed of a large number of people who infrequently visit the courthouse as witnesses, litigants and spectators. The circulation routes and spaces used by each group must be studied, and additional information on user expectations obtained by questionnaires and interviews, and by consultation with the staff who deal with the public in each department. The following guidelines are useful to the consideration of public convenience and satisfaction:

▪ Functions serving large numbers of people should be grouped on the lower floors of the courthouse. In addition to elevators, an open stair or escalator should be used to provide direct communication between these floors.

▪ An information booth should be located at the main entrance to the courthouse, and at other locations, such as the jury assembly room and witness lounge, where large numbers of people gather.

▪ A clearly legible, color-coded system of directories and signs should be prominently displayed. The location of offices, courtrooms, witness lounges, jury assembly rooms, toilets, information stations, vending machines, snack bars and telephones must be indicated.

▪ Spaces for a wide variety of activities such as reading, working, conversation, games and watching television should be provided in jury assembly rooms and witness lounges.

A voice amplification system should be provided in all large courtrooms to assure that the public and press can hear the proceedings. Comfortable seats and coat racks are also necessary in the spectator area.

At this point, a cautionary note must be sounded, for it is all too easy to become preoccupied with technology, operations research and long-range trends and projections, and to overlook the physical and psychological well-being of the staff and public in the courthouse building. This human factor, with which the fourth planning guideline is finally concerned, is difficult to articulate with precision, but it must be considered. The problem is more than simply choosing comfortable chairs and providing sufficient toilets. A basic question must be asked: "What kind of human environment is best for the particular transactions that take place?" Factors like the absence of noise and distraction, adequate and comfortable lighting, convenient places to sit while waiting, and windows in areas where they will be most appreciated must be considered in order to assure that each space is comfortable and pleasant, and well suited to its particular function. The architect and the building committee, moreover, must take specific steps to gather information on user needs by in-depth interviews with courthouse staff, who should be asked to study the plans and models and suggest improvements.

The new New Haven County Courthouse is a monumentally simple building. Its limestone facade, built close to the sidewalk, continues the line of one of New Haven's major streets (photo opposite page). The main entrance is at the corner of the building (photo right), and it leads into a large ground-floor lobby with public elevators and a reception desk (plan below). General offices are on this floor. The courtroom floors above are arranged according to the vertical circulation scheme described on the previous page—with small private lobbies (and private elevators) generally serving pairs of courtrooms. The private elevators also reach the jury assembly room on the top floor. A law library is on the next to the top floor, and is shown in the photo below right.

NEW HAVEN COUNTY COURTHOUSE, New Haven, Connecticut. Architects: *William F. Pedersen & Associates, Inc.—project architects: William F. Pedersen, Fred B. Bookhart, Jr., David M. Chin and John W. Persse.* Engineers: *Macchi & Hoffman* (structural), *Technical Design Associates* (mechanical/electrical). Consultant: *Allan Greenberg,* (Connecticut Judicial Department). General contractor: *Dwight Building Company.*

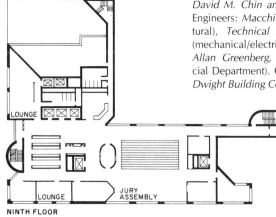

NINTH FLOOR

FOURTH FLOOR

FIRST FLOOR

10

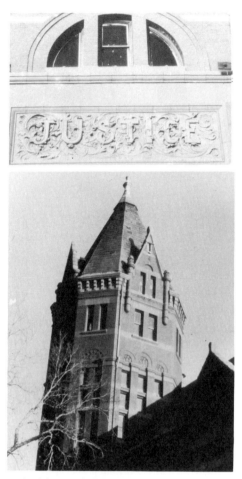

Details of the Marshall County Courthouse in Marysville, Kansas, one of nine Midwestern county courthouses selected for feasibility studies at the University of Illinois Chicago Circle Campus.

Courtroom in the Warren County Courthouse, Warrenton, Missouri. Below, Trumpeters of Justice adorning the clock tower of the Stark County Courthouse in Canton, Ohio.

The county courthouse: rediscovering a national asset

by Ben Weese

It is appropriate in a time of growing historic interest to study the American courthouse as a functioning building type of the highest symbolic order. Certainly no other building type has such wide-spread impact on local history, because of its monumental quality and its location, which make it a real symbol of the physical and social organization of countless American communities.

During the last half of the nineteenth century and the first few years of the twentieth, particularly fine court buildings were erected by many counties, especially in the Midwest, which was just then coming into its own economically as well as politically. The county's judicial and administrative offices were housed in a centrally located building in each county seat. Thus county seats were important locations, and the courthouse was carefully sited on the highest hill or the most prominent central square where often their cupolas and towers could be seen from the farthest reaches of the county. In their pomp and style, the courthouses represented a visual locus surrounded by the region's chief commercial buildings. It is because of these factors that the monumental older courthouse cannot be replaced, for without it the town itself loses definition and cohesion.

During the past ten years, nevertheless, we have lost scores of these majestic structures. Throughout the Midwest, noble and opulent reminders of the civic pride of our forebears have fallen to the wrecking ball. Numerous courthouses are threatened today, and more will become endangered in the next few years.

On the surface, there are two reasons for the recent number of courthouse preservation problems. In many cases, generations of deferred maintenance have finally taken their toll, and the buildings have developed serious code violations as well as deplorably seedy appearances. Oftentimes, however, maintenance-related problems are cosmetic in nature, and comparatively easily remedied when objectively approached.

More serious are problems caused by the changing functions of modern county government, coupled with rising county population. Courthouse architects of the nineteenth century could not foresee the changes which have taken place in recent years in county services. Buildings which quite adequately housed governmental services of county courts, clerks, recorders and tax offices are today stretched to the bursting point by the addition of county health departments, welfare offices, motor vehicle license offices, veterans' affairs offices and agricultural extension agents. Some counties in the path of urbanization have added personnel to the point where the old building is overwhelmed.

Ben Weese, of Harry Weese & Associates in Chicago, is an architect who energetically champions old buildings of all kinds, and also designs new ones.

Nevertheless, why is one county able to rearrange and accommodate its growth and changing needs in a refurbished old courthouse, while another with identical problems ends up replacing its majestic showpiece, its monumental heart, with a faceless, standardized one-story office building devoid of civic dignity? The very fact that this is happening in some counties and not in others calls for more coordinated study of a problem which lends itself to literally thousands of analogous situations, not just in the Midwest but throughout the entire country.

It is our contention that the key element in the preservation of courthouses is the attitude of the architect and the people involved. For too long, architects and citizens have looked at these older buildings as white elephants—liabilities instead of assets. It takes imagination to find solutions to the vexing problem of accommodating modern needs in an older space, and too often architects have taken the easier path of starting from scratch. But in an age of increasing visual standardization in which we are daily losing our sense of time and place, we must begin to find ways to keep our very important landmarks.

This, then, was the rationale behind the Historic Courthouse Project, a cooperative effort involving the National Endowment for the Arts, the National Trust for Historic Preservation, the University of Illinois Chicago Circle Campus and Harry Weese & Associates. Over 1000 counties in 13 Midwestern states were surveyed and asked to participate in the study. From the responses, we were able to narrow the scope of the project to a study of courthouse space management in counties experiencing both increasing and decreasing growth. We elected not to become involved in eleventh-hour hopeless cases, nor was stylistic excellence a major factor in the selection process. While each possesses its individual problems, all nine courthouses chosen for intensive study represent fairly typical conditions, so the results should have wide application everywhere.

Each courthouse was assigned to teams of fourth- and fifth-year architecture students at UICC, acting as "paraprofessionals" under the supervision of a group of professional advisors, including Mr. Michael Lisec and myself, of Harry Weese & Associates.

Prior to the teams' field visits to the subject courthouses for interviews and on-site investigations, the entire group made a joint field trip to seven counties in Illinois to develop a background understanding of the problem. Team visits to the selected courthouses involved interviews with all county officials, on-site photography and data gathering, meetings with local historical societies, interested individuals and inevitably the local media. A wealth of data was brought home, sorted and weighed, and mutual problems were compared. Repeat trips were made when necessary. One county required a special visit by Don Anderson, of The Engineers Collabo-

Marshall County Courthouse, Marysville, Kansas

UICC students Richard Latkowski and Gerhard Rosenberg, under the direction of Ben Weese (and with the advice of The Engineers Collaborative, Ltd.), developed a renovation proposal for the Marshall County Courthouse that, according to current growth projections, will be able to satisfy the County's space needs through 1990. The study, which advocates a versatile adaptive use rather than precise historical reconstruction, begins with a thorough replanning of existing floors in the building, and then proposes either the construction of new annexes or a conversion of existing adjacent buildings to accommodate ultimate space requirements.

The Courthouse, which was built in 1891, is a brick and sandstone faced structure with terra cotta trim, and it was designed by the Milwaukee architectural firm of Henry C. Koch and Company.

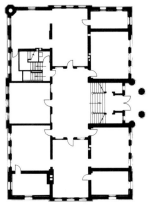

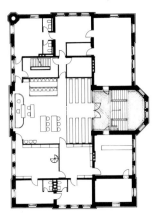

rative, our consultant structural engineer. The students were then asked to develop preservation action strategies which could be returned to their para-clients, the county commissioners, as completed feasibility studies.

Although in the beginning these architecture students were not necessarily committed or interested in questions of preservation strategy, they have made a very mature response to a complex, difficult, and sometimes negative situation. These 19 emerging professionals have received their first in-depth training in a highly skilled but largely uncharted area: that of professional architectural preservationist. The training they have received will help them meet the growing demand for knowledgeable and sympathetic professionals in this field.

One of the chief goals of this effort was to find out what it will cost to save buildings. Unwise counsel in the past has called for major surgery that bankrupts and compromises the patient beyond recognition.

Rule One is that the old building, con-

structed in an era of cheap labor and high quality craftsmanship, was better built than new buildings, given reasonable maintenance (or even none!). Old buildings withstand the test of time.

Rule Two is to not intervene beyond what program and common sense require. Naturally, accommodations to public safety and codes must be made, but an overzealous effort at "sanitizing," automatically dropping ceilings, closing off the grand stair or the central cupola are misguided. "Compensatory" code requirements can be negotiated so that public safety, access for the handicapped, etc., can be accommodated without losing the original grandeur and concept of the building. Minimal intervention is a hallmark of a competitive final cost.

As mentioned earlier, it is possible for court functions to continue to be accommodated in these buildings. In some cases, however, a series of unplanned changes over the years had resulted in too much space devoted to dead storage (election machines, old

records, etc.) or completely unused areas such as attics. Here, a comprehensive plan was developed that focused on the total space available. Minimal alterations resulted in greatly increased space. In other cases, light steel mezzanine floors were added between floors (often 10-20 feet clear) with no structural problems, because of the massive masonry walls.

A word here about extensively modifying the interiors of an historic building: in many counties all the resources were spent on the exterior shell and thus the buildings have virtually no internal decor. In these cases sympathetic embellishment is appropriate to sensibly renovate a building. In general, exterior maintenance on these axial, symmetrical buildings is the prime need. Most often additions—unless underground or sensibly linked—are a defacement. In all our records and data on courthouses, we cannot unqualifiedly recommend one successful example of an addition.

In the first place, expansion should be considered within the interior of the courthouse itself through better space utilization,

Warren County Courthouse, Warrenton, Missouri

In their feasibility study for the renovation of this building, students David Lencioni and Wayne Miller first tackled minor structural problems like a sagging second floor and a wobbly cupola on the roof. Then they turned to replanning the space inside, and to developing a courthouse "campus" plan by renovating the buildings on Warrenton's Main Street. They confidently predict that the county's space requirements can be met in this way.

Stark County Courthouse, Canton, Ohio

Because of the unusual enthusiasm with which their initial feasibility study was greeted by county officials, students Robert Klute, Thomas Meredith and John Pohl continued their work and submitted a second-phase proposal in March 1975, and a final proposal in June, 1975.

The Stark County Courthouse, as the adjacent photographs attest, has already gone through a series of renovations. The original building was begun in 1868; by 1893 it was no longer large enough to accommodate all of the court and clerical functions of this growing county, and it was more or less completely remodeled by Cleveland architect George F. Hammond. Further minor alterations brought the building to its pre-renovation state.

Klute, Meredith and Pohl's scheme called for preservation and restoration of the building's exterior, its main lobby and at least one courtroom; the remainder of the interior would be remodeled in a contemporary manner. All county functions not directly related to the courts would be removed from the courthouse and housed in existing adjacent buildings or new ones.

mezzanine construction, or attic expansion. Secondly, many county services unrelated to the traditional court functions do not have to be housed under one roof and can easily be physically separated. This is the basis for the "campus" concept, already practiced successfully by numerous counties throughout the country. Through this method, counties expand into available nearby commercial buildings which are often themselves of architectural merit. This commitment to the traditional central downtown location is critical, for the alternative is to move to the edge of town or to an off-center location where the whole pattern of historic community growth is abandoned and a devastating suburbanizing influence takes hold. Gone is the memorable image of the majestically imposing building, replaced by a courthouse, which is easily confused with any new shopping center.

With an arsenal of strategies, a sympathetic "client/user," and a dedicated and sensitive professional, I submit that the clarification and solution of the courthouse problem is possible. In our Bicentennial era, it is the American people who benefit from the daily presence of the historic courthouse as a continuing symbol of our heritage of justice and democratic government.

This joint project involving the University of Illinois Chicago Circle Campus, Harry Weese and Associates, and the National Trust for Historic Preservation represents the first attempt to find broadly applicable answers to a wide-spread problem: making the grand, impractical and extravagant courthouse of another era suitable for the vastly changed conditions of modern life. The results of the study clearly show that most courthouses can be preserved if people are motivated. But county commissioners are a conservative lot who generally have little experience or understanding of historic preservation. They rely on their paid expert, the architect, to render a professional judgment. We hope the methods we have developed will motivate both architects and county officials to explore fully and imaginatively all possible ways in which the architectural gems of the past can remain in service for the future.

As important as the preservation of these civic monuments is the sensitizing of the student architects to view the architectural extravagances of the past as essential anchors to keep us steady in an ocean of prefabbed standardization. Even if they are never involved again in a courthouse, the students who participated in this exercise have had their eyes opened to the possibilities for imaginative reuse of many older buildings to enrich the fabric of our lives.

To call further attention to the preservation of historic courthouses, county officials and architects were invited to a national conference on the subject, sponsored by the National Trust in December 1975, and a summary publication of the project results was published for wide distribution in 1976. Perhaps the emphasis that was put on the noble ambitions of previous generations during the Bicentennial years will stimulate all of us to assure the preservation of our temples of justice.

CHAPTER TWO

BUILDINGS FOR PUBLIC SERVICES: FIREHOUSES, POST OFFICES, POLICE STATIONS, JAILS AND A MAINTENANCE STRUCTURE

Like the buildings for the basic function of government in the last chapter, the buildings that are needed to provide those basic services that we expect from governments are sometimes an integral part of our towns and cities. In fact—now that those other buildings are often in somewhat isolated centers—buildings such as firehouses and police stations are by the nature of their required disbursement through the community, a more integral part of our main steets. Accordingly, the differences in an appropriate response to the surrounding environment should be and can be pronounced—as seen in this chapter in the case of two police stations in the same city, New York. The characters of architects Gruzen & Partners' downtown Police Headquarters building and architects Holden/Yang/Raemsch/Terjesen's 114th Precinct Station are about as different as night and day—or as different as both characters are from that of architect William Morgan's Jacksonville police headquarters. Yet, each building is a carefully thought-through response to its environment and to the role that it plays. Each fits in with the buildings around it. The New York headquarters is monumental—like those classic-style municipal headquarters adjacent to it. And its site development weds those older thoroughbreds into a more humane locale. The 114th street precinct building is all function, while its stolid mass blends into the local neighborhood's low buildings. And the Jacksonville building is something else, a revolutionary approach to supplying basic needs in an environment that is far more elevated than basic.

Similarly, the differences in the firehouses shown in this chapter speak of a wide range of influences and ideas. In Victoria, British Columbia, architects Orme & Levinson's firehouse is modest in its presentations—but makes a strong sculptural statement. Architects Venturi and Rauch's New Haven fire station is also strong—but in a cerebral sense, that may not necessarily be appealing to the uninitiated. Unlike the other two examples, San Francisco's Engine Company Number 14 fits simply into a row of urban houses, and might be missed if not sought.

All of the buildings in this chapter give strong visual messages—with modest strength where appropriate. And they are hence all the more important.

PURE FUNCTIONALISM CREATES STRIKING FORM

The prime concern of a fireman is to respond quickly to an alarm in order to save property and lives, and a well designed fire station is one in which the planning decisions are predicated on that function. This new station, located in a suburb of Victoria, British Columbia, was designed with that in mind—it is totally functional and efficient, and from that grows its design quality. The most dominant form on the site is a unique 45-foot-high concrete practice/training tower. By its nature, and the nature of the site, it could not be screened from view, so the architects made it an integral feature of the station and designed it to be sculptural as well as functional.

d'Estrubé Industrial Photography photos

TOWER

FIRE HALL

N

SOUTH ELEVATION

The tower's sculptural nature is here silhouetted through an apparatus-bay door. In the dormitory (lower left) folding beds allow the room to be converted into a lecture hall for training and community education programs. The apparatus floor (lower right) is open, free of posts which could become obstacles to firemen running to trucks in an emergency. Its high, unobstructed ceiling can accommodate the newest equipment. To increase this area's use, light fixtures were placed so light would fall on work area between trucks, and the bay is heated on a separate zone. Recessed open closets permit quick access to "turn out" gear—helmets, boots and coats. Speakers throughout the station relay alarm information; and an intercom system notifies men in training area.

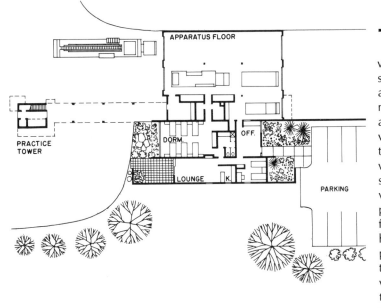

APPARATUS FLOOR

PRACTICE
TOWER

DORM | OFF.

LOUNGE | K. | PARKING

The practice/training tower simulates a multi-story building, with typical window openings, a sloping roof, high parapets, open and enclosed stairways, balconies, a "break through" door, and an open shaft used to simulate elevator shaft fires and smoke inhalation escapes. A 60-foot covered walkway, connecting tower and station is not only an important visual element, but provides a protected place for rolling the 50-foot lengths of hose and—with its high parapet—is used for ladder practice. The area surrounding the tower drains to a sump pump which recycles water during practice sessions and times of community water rationing. The shape of the site, the desire to save the only tree on it, and the need for maneuvering room around the tower de-

termined the linear nature of the station. While the extension wall (right in plan, photo lower left) visually reinforces this, it also separates the parking area, giving a clear path for fire engines responding to an alarm. Roof heights step down following the function of space, from the 16-foot-high drive-through apparatus bay, to 14-foot-high ambulance/workshop bay, to 11-foot-high dormitory/lecture hall, to 8-foot-high ceiling in lounge area. Two short perpendicular corridors connect lounge and all living quarters to the apparatus bay for efficient access to trucks.

SAANICH FIRE HALL NO. 3, near Victoria, British Columbia. Architects: *Orme & Levinson.* Engineers: *Graeme & Murray Consultants Ltd.* (structural for tower); *B. W. Brooker Engineering Ltd.* (mechanical/plumbing); *Spratt & Associates Ltd.* (electrical). Contractor: *Dura Construction Ltd.*

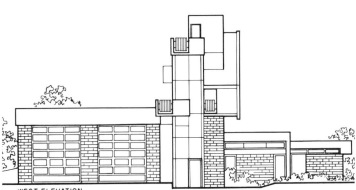

WEST ELEVATION

SAN FRANCISCO FIREHOUSE

This building was one of four prize winners in a field of 130 designs submitted in a municipal competition held in San Francisco. The competition was unusual in that the jury was charged with selecting four designs for premiation and then selecting the architect of one as the candidate for appointment by the city to be the architect for the first in a series of new firehouses. The authors of the other premiated schemes would, by implication, be commissioned for later firehouses. The jury pointed out that the principle of selecting an architect, rather than a design, for such a program had great merit, because of the complexity of the problem and the likelihood that no competition solution would be completely

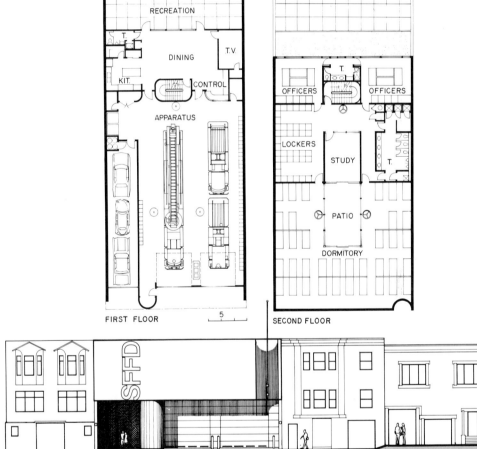

Barbeau Engh photos

RECREATION

DINING

T.V.

KIT.

CONTROL

APPARATUS

T.

FIRST FLOOR 5

OFFICERS   OFFICERS

T.

LOCKERS   STUDY   T.

PATIO

DORMITORY

SECOND FLOOR

ELEVATION

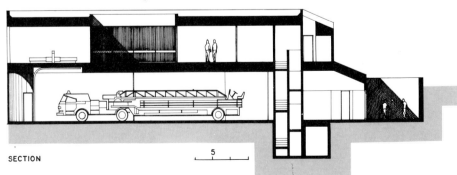

SECTION 5

adequate without additional, highly technical modification. The building shown here, by the firm of Braccia/De Brer/Heglund, is thus somewhat different from the design which was originally submitted, though its formal outlines are the same. A remarkably simple facade fronts the street between two row houses, and from it the fire engines can emerge at a moment's notice. The lower floor of the building contains, in addition, communal facilities.

SAN FRANCISCO ENGINE COMPANY #14, San Francisco, California. Architects: *Braccia/De Brer/Heglund—Jacques De Brer,* partner in charge of design. Engineers: *Harding-Lawson Associates* (soils), *Yanow & Bauer* (mechanical/electrical). General contractor: *Dunn & Gaulke Construction Co.*

For a sprawling urban renewal site in New Haven's Dixwell neighborhood, Venturi and Rauch were asked to plan a home for three formerly separate fire companies and a rescue unit. The result is a box within a box—the smaller one being a two-story "apparatus room" for fire engines and other equipment, and the larger one the almost-square building itself, which contains the apparatus room and everything else.

The big doors face neither of the two intersecting streets, but open instead onto the angled lane that connects them. This arrangement, and a wide apron, assures optimum maneuverability for trucks headed in either direction. It also assures, however, that the building does not face the major street (to the right in the large photo, opposite). Thus the building is truncated on this major street to provide a pedestrian entrance.

Above the entrance a brick wall that carries a long list of company names sails out into space. Most of the building is finished in a dense, but unglazed, brick with matching mortar; it produces a heightened version of common brick red, saturated enough to recall "fire engine red" in a city whose fire engines are white. Standard, natural finish aluminum windows and storefront glazing are used. But there are also special elements, in addition to the brick sign, to identify this as a public building: a flagpole set in a tiny but lush green lawn, and a small white marble veneer wall that marks the pedestrian entrance.

The carefully maintained, like-new look of the interiors is striking in combination with the like-old look of the finishes, which recall a standard institutional interior of the 1950s: light green glazed wall tile, marbleized floor tile in a checkerboard pattern, rubber cove bases and natural, colored aluminum hardware. Within this vocabulary there are small but noticeable shifts from the ordinary, combined with unusual precision in detail.

DIXWELL FIRE STATION, New Haven, Connecticut. Architects: *Venturi and Rauch—Robert Venturi, John Rauch, Arthur Jones, Leslie DeLong, Robert Renfro.* Engineers: *The Keast and Hood Company* (structural); *Vinokur-Pace Engineering Services, Inc.* (mechanical/electrical). Consultants: *Dian Boone* (interiors); *William Gennetti* (cost). Contractor: *J. H. Hogan.*

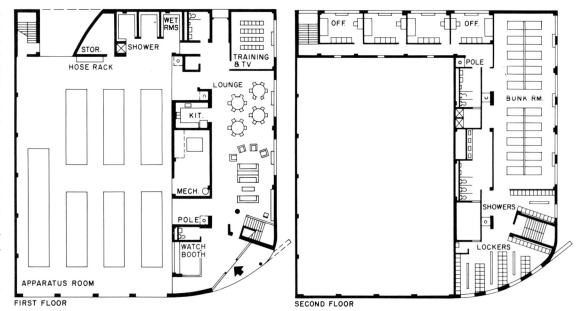

FIRST FLOOR

SECOND FLOOR

Cervin Robinson photos

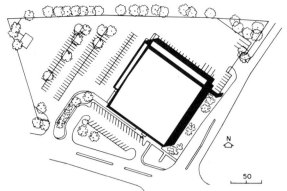

A NEW REGIONAL PROTOTYPE DESIGNED FOR THE U.S. POSTAL SERVICE EMERGES IN THE SOUTHEAST

What started as a single facility—a regional process and distribution center for Florence, South Carolina—has now become three. Nearly identical structures are now complete in Fort Myers, Florida, McAllen, Texas, and Gulfport, Mississippi. Others may follow. All are the work of architects/engineers Lyles, Bissett, Carlisle & Wolff. The sketch below hints at the character of these buildings. They are industial in function but not in flavor. They are adaptable to a variety of flat, suburban sites. Most important, they represent a significant design departure for a major Federal agency—a quest for high quality, contempory design within a realistic budget that deserves every encouragement it can get.

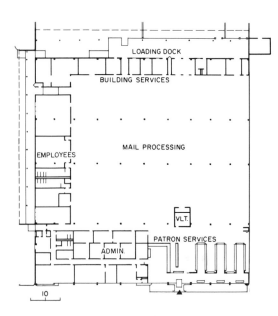

LOADING DOCK

BUILDING SERVICES

MAIL PROCESSING

EMPLOYEES

VLT.

ADMIN.

PATRON SERVICES

10

"The objectives set for these prototype designs," says design director John Paul McGowan of LBC&W, were that they should be clean, handsome, economical buildings, built with industrial components and technology, but non-industrial in character. They were to provide the community with a new type of Federal building, one that is straightforward and non-monumental, and one that is well sited and landscaped."

The Fort Myers facility, shown above, is typical in its development of these objectives. Like the others, it is a pre-engineered, light steel frame, clad in a four-inch, foam-filled metal panel, finished in porcelain and flush mounted to the structural frame. Bay sizes, spans and column dimensions were selected to conform with the several systems now on the

market. The generic plan is almost square and contains approximately 50,000 square feet. Within this volume, the largest space is set aside for mail processing—a 33,000-square-foot workroom of automated and semi-automated processing equipment that operates 24 hours a day. Flanking this space on three sides are small work spaces, employee service spaces, and a small patron area that functions as a local post office. The fourth side of the vast work space is kept open for purposes of future expansion. In this event, exterior panels can be easily dismantled, then remounted to enclose a new bay. Truck loading docks wrap around two sides of the structure for convenient servicing by various kinds of Post Office vehicles from neighborhood runabouts to giant trailers.

The buildings are not frontal in the way

that so many post offices used to be. The public is led to the main entry by brightly-painted hand rails and enters under a metal canopy also painted a bright red-orange (photo above). These rails are steel pipes, bent around corners of narrow radius without any visible deformation of their circular section. Rails and canopy are bright accents against an otherwise white facade, a welcome moment of color intoxication in an otherwise sober composition. Behind these rails are floor-to-ceiling, tinted glass window walls that mark the limits of the public areas. A strip of quarry tile reinforces those limits and unites inside and out.

The Postal Service authorized the development of new counters, writing desks and display cases. These were designed in plywood by the architects and faced in plastic laminate.

A light-gray vinyl is the prototypical wall covering. This palette of materials was selected for durability and ease of maintenance as well as for modest construction cost which was well below average—even including landscaping—over the three projects.

The success of these structures, derives from the design quality obtained from simple, industrial components used in a clear-headed way with an eye to scale, to detail, and to pleasant massing. Of at least equal interest is the decision by the Postal Service to seek a pre-engineered, prototypical building form. The existing inventory of sectional center facilities like these, though wrapped in different skins to suit particular site surroundings, mostly have the same plan, spatial dispositions and volumes. What is different about the new, pre-engineered structures is that design and construction times have been dramatically reduced. And in view of the fact that the activity of mail processing, whether carried on in Texas, Florida or South Carolina, is virtually identical, a strong case is made for building replication.

Yet another pre-engineered center, by a different architect, is underway in Garland, Texas, and others will almost certainly follow. If their design quality remains as high as at Florence, where the new facility won a State AIA design award, they will welcome additions to the light industrial sites to which they are adapted.

The architect's fee for the Center at Florence was negotiated and fell within the normal range for buildings of this type. In spite

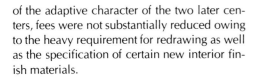

George C. Grigg photos

of the adaptive character of the two later centers, fees were not substantially reduced owing to the heavy requirement for redrawing as well as the specification of certain new interior finish materials.

POSTAL SECTIONAL CENTER FACILITY AND AN-NEXES, Florence, South Carolina, Fort Myers, Florida and McAllen, Texas. Owner: *U.S. Postal Service, Southern Region*—Bill Wright, general manager, Design and Construction Division. Architects/engineers: *LBC&W of South Carolina*—John McGowan, director of design; Jerry F. Friedner, project architect. Associate architects: *W.R. Frizzell Associates* (for Fort Myers), *Rike & Ogden, Architects* (for McAllen). Contractors: *Ruscon Construction Company* (for Florence); *B.E. Beecroft Company, Inc.* (for McAllen); *Dawson Construction Company* (for Fort Myers).

SCHENECTADY POLICE HEADQUARTERS

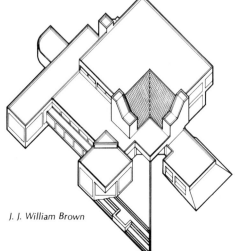

J. J. William Brown

Joseph W. Molitor photos

This police headquarters building—designed by architects Werner Feibes and James Schmitt—was built to accommodate the activities of a 150-person police force, and also to create a handsome and visible image for the law enforcement profession in this upstate New York town of 81,000 people. The site is adjacent to the Schenectady County Public Library and close by the central business district, city hall and post office, since it was thought that such continuity with the everyday public life and affairs of the community would aid the morale of the police force even as it indicated to the public the force's role.

The form of the building, according to the architects, resulted from the complexity of activities that make up a modern law-enforcement facility; they allowed each of these elements proper expression and then organized them all in their most natural and immediately identifiable way, so that, according to Schmitt, the building "emerged as a village cluster of interconnected forms." The diagram on the right shows how security areas, administrative areas and public areas are related.

SCHENECTADY POLICE HEADQUARTERS, Schenectady, New York. Architects: *Feibes & Schmitt.* Engineers: *John T. Percy and Associates* (structural); *Robert D. Krouner Consulting Engineer* (mechanical/electrical); *Thomsen Associates* (soils). Consultant: *Briston, Hiser & Leaver* (landscape). General contractor: *Hanson Construction Corporation.*

PUBLIC
STAFF
SECURITY

Lower Manhattan's new Police Headquarters, with its beguiling pedestrian plaza (glimpsed through the arch below) was commissioned nearly two decades ago. In 1974, two mayors, six police commissioners and nine public works commissioners later, the building was complete and occupied. Through all these administrative changes, with their inevitable but vexing delays, architects Gruzen & Partners were the only continuing presence. Their patience and determination resulted on not only a splendid building but, perhaps even more important, in a sound and coherent piece of civic planning in a portion of the city where this virtue has been absent too long.

The photo above shows the office of the present police commissioner who sits at a desk once used by Theodore Roosevelt when he held the same post at the end of the last century.

Typical office space (photo left and plan below) is designed for flexible clerical use and is laid out generously around an efficient central core. The small courtroom (photo below), is one of two such spaces used for intra-departmental trials and/or hearings. Wood panel walls, parquet floors, especially nice furnishings and double-height ceiling give the space a high level of finish and express its organizational importance.

During the selection of finishes, the architects argued that exposed concrete in ceiling coffers and columns should be left unpainted to simplify the building's maintenance. They lost. All these surfaces, for better or worse, are painted—mostly in a light beige. A variable air volume system, with registers concealed by the lighting, is used here for the first time in a public building in New York and gives the Police Headquarters a "fine-tuning" capacity that is significant in terms of energy efficiency.

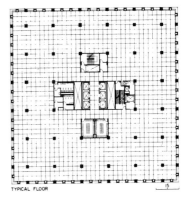

TYPICAL FLOOR

Chambers Street is a stop on Manhattan's West Side subway. Climbing to the street, up stairs softly frescoed in grime, the visitor finds himself near the intersection of Chambers and Centre Streets under the broad vaulting of McKim, Mead & White's colossal Municipal Building. This exuberant, faintly Italianate civic skyscraper, completed in 1914, houses a large chunk of the city's civil service. In a welcoming gesture, its colonnaded front opens, through an heroic central arch, to the southeast and now reveals New York's recently completed Police Headquarters Building and Pedestrian Plaza.

The 75-foot-wide pedestrian plaza, designed by Gruzen & Partners with M. Paul Friedberg & Associates, is so carefully planted that the visitor scarcely realizes he is on a bridge with a busy traffic artery—Park Row—cutting underneath. Strongly axial, the plaza is lined with honey locust trees and fitted with benches, a large sculpture executed in weathering steel by Bernard Rosenthal, and a variety of small pedestrian amenities that encourage strollers to pause, lovers to dally, city brownbaggers to linger over sandwiches and apples.

This grand space, with its seductive pedestrian ambience, seems so entirely appropriate that it is hard, in retrospect, to imagine that planners and police officials at first opposed its creation, favoring instead a narrow aerial tunnel reaching up, over Park Row and down again on the other side. The decision to depress Park Row and create the present plaza was agonizing. It required the shifting of several approach ramps to the Brooklyn Bridge. That meant the cooperation of a spate of city agencies and a helping hand from the Office of Lower Manhattan Development—as well as all the patience and persuasive powers the architects (and designer Peter Samton in particular) could muster. That the effort was worth it can no longer be doubted. Not only are the plaza spaces and subspaces handsome in themselves (though they show signs of hard use), but they bring to the edge of this civic district an amenity and a planning coherence it has long lacked. The Police Department is now physically and symbolically linked to the residential neighborhood to the south as well as to the courthouses along Centre Street—instead of being estranged from both in unapproachable, arterial limbo. The building itself sits squarely on its irregularly-shaped site. The main entrance is on axis with the Municipal Building and is recessed under the cantilever of the

tower. The lowest levels contain a large public parking garage (478 cars), pistol range, detention cells, equipment stores and a host of specialized police spaces. The plaza level includes main lobby, the Department of Licenses, press and public spaces and a large assembly hall (photo opposite) hung with banners. by Sheila White Samton. These spaces thrust outward in all directions forming low projections over which the ten-story cube of office spaces rises abruptly. Tower and base are both clad in brick, but the separation between them is clearly articulated by massive concrete trusses—that become walls inside—and that distribute the tower loads to heavy columns spaced on 30-foot centers. The regularized grid of window openings in the tower is nicely detailed in deep reveals and stands in contrast to the more or less windowless façades of the lower elements. A deep band of brick forms the parapet on all sides and conceals a mechanical penthouse and a helistop on the roof.

If the tower offices are rather ordinary, the lobby, assembly hall and trial rooms are decidedly extraordinary. These are the prime spaces and the designers, as the photos reveal, have worked to bring these spaces to a high level of civic design.

New York has sometimes seemed a city intent on leaching its future away in fragmented, ad hoc planning decisions. That it has not happened here at the new Civic Plaza is a cause for some rejoicing. Part of the credit must go to the Department of Public Works who acted as client and, by prearrangement with the architects, assumed responsibility for construction supervision. Partial credit is also due the Police Department who assessed their needs realistically and were not afraid to open their "front porch" to large crowds and the wider community. Finally, credit is due Gruzen & Partners who never gave up on the City, when others did, and who persevered to create an intelligently planned, unifying and dignified addition to New York's Civic Center against what many would reckon as formidable odds.

Bettina Cirone

POLICE HEADQUARTERS, PEDESTRIAN PLAZA AND PARKING GARAGE, New York City. Architects: *Gruzen & Partners—Jordan Gruzen, executive director; Peter Samton, design director; Charles Silverman, production director.* Engineers: *Farkas Barron & Partners* (structural); *Joseph R. Loring & Associates* (mechanical). Landscape architects: *M. Paul Friedberg & Associates.* Contractor: *Castagna & Son.*

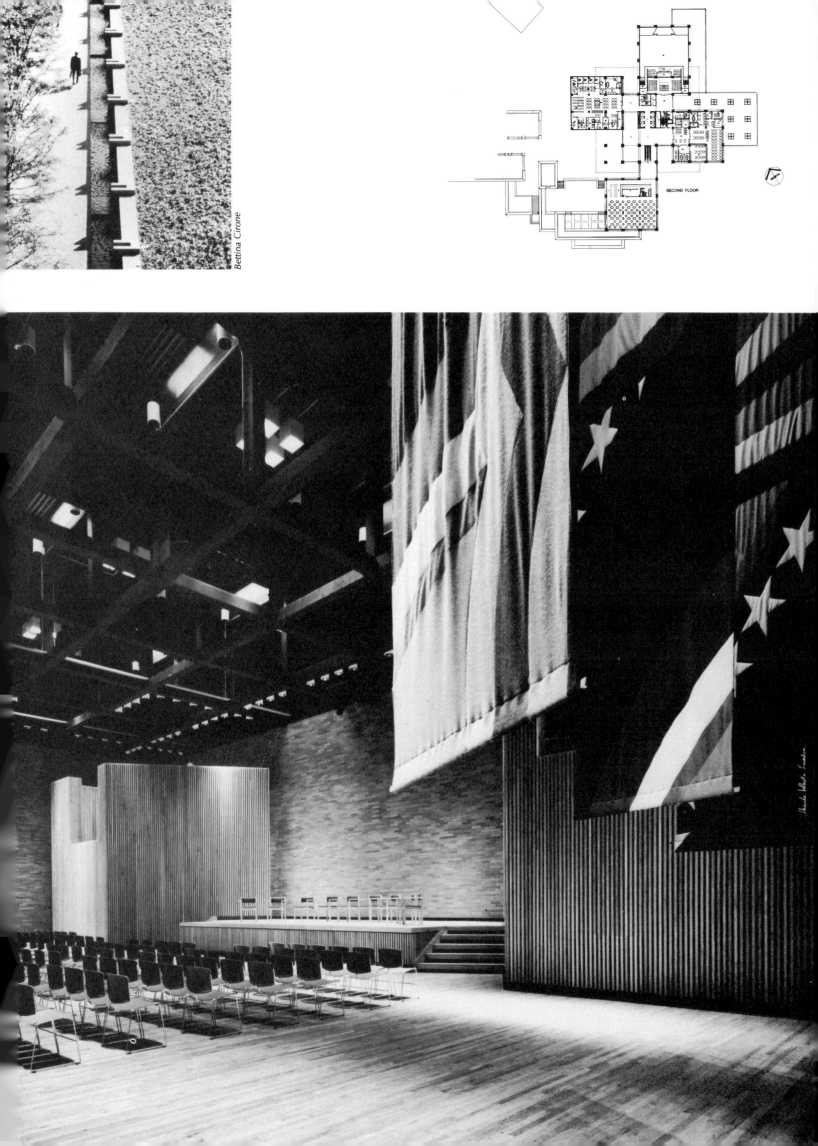

Bettina Cirone

SECOND FLOOR

BREAKING DOWN THE BATTLEMENTS: JACKSONVILLE'S NEW POLICE HEADQUARTERS

In designing what is officially known as the Police Memorial Building in Jacksonville, Florida, architect William Morgan has produced two unified civic facilities that would seem by traditional standards to be incompatible: a functioning law enforcement agency and a public park. But it is exactly this skillful marriage of the two normally distinct faces of government's responsibility that makes this building significant. The park is located on the stepped levels of the agency's roof, and it lends a totally new and humane image to normally stern and forbidding functions. But such innovation is nothing new to Morgan. The two-part use of the site is consistent with his innovative design approaches for all sorts of buildings (see the last page of this description.) Morgan's buildings are in harmony with their surroundings—or sometimes with what their surroundings might be in the most considerate of worlds. Truly, he is telling us something about the nature of what architecture can be all about—and in this case what government might be all about.

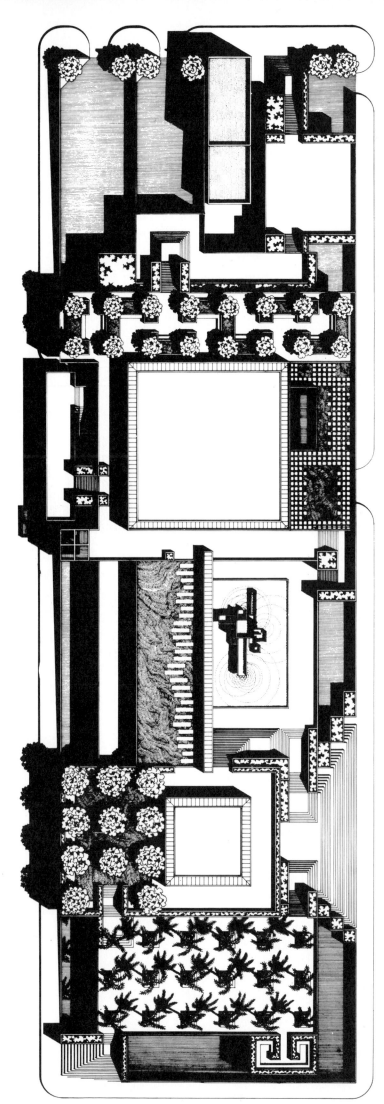

In the past, some police stations have been designed as civic monuments (in the spirit of the great nineteenth century railroad stations), others as examples of hardheaded efficiency. It requires an appreciation of both design approaches, and it requires the spirit of the most recent times, to produce the adventurous design shown here by architect William Morgan for Jacksonville, Florida's Police Memorial Building.

First of all, the building is monumental—but in two very different senses from the overbearing connotation of that description. It is a monument to a new concept of civic responsibility, wherein the barriers between government's function and the aim of that function, human amenity, are broken down. The building is monumental because its symbolic values go far beyond its day-to-day purposes, and boost humane sensibilities. (Another monumental quality is the visual recall of the ancient Indian architecture of northern Florida—a subject that has fascinated Morgan for many years.)

The design was the winner of a competition sponsored by the AIA, and the jury report stated that the selection was based on the need for breaking down the barriers of isolation, unpleasantness and resentment that have recently become attached to the image of law enforcement. In an understatement, the jury said "we tried to choose a design with an airy rather than eerie atmosphere." The jury also said that the design was selected for visible "ease of approach *and* efficiency in handling day-to-day business."

And the building does handle business. Police functions are distributed over two floors, which are elevated above a subgrade parking area. The parking level also accommodates service functions such as mechanical equipment rooms, and provides space for future expansion of the building. (The utilization of the current 208,000-square-foot building is approximately 70 per cent). The main floor is surprisingly straightforward in plan for a building with apparently complicated volumes that are seen from the exterior. All spaces are organized around two interior courts, which are respectively centers of public-related and internal functions. Accordingly, the main entrance (see photos previous page) leads to the smaller court (see section), around which are public services and records, and facilities for public transaction—such as paying parking tickets. The sheriff's office and the offices of other police officers are located around the larger court, along with such functions as detention.

Architect Morgan was determined to create a building in which people's sense of location would be quick and easy, as they traveled from place to place. Accordingly, the two courts are connected by a two-story-high gallery (photo top). Here hang banners created by artist Anne Emanuel, whose designs are derived from paintings by local school children transferred onto canvas. The building's exterior walls (as seen in the photo above) are poured-in-place concrete with a fluted, bush hammered finish that is interrupted by smooth concrete bands at the floor levels.

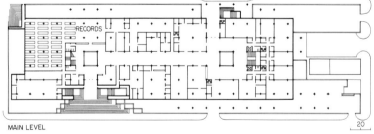

MAIN LEVEL

UPPER LEVEL

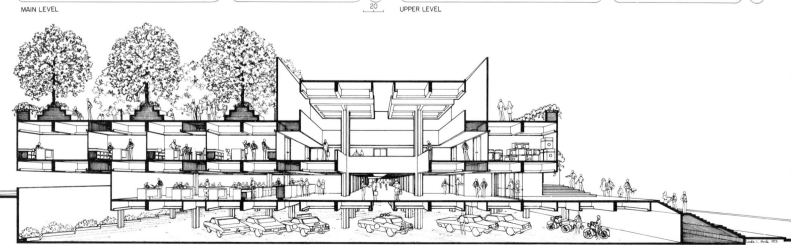

Despite the building's open appearance, security was a strong consideration in the design. Accordingly, there are few windows, and skylights take on great importance. The skylights are located over the two courts and the connecting gallery. The larger court rises four stories from the parking level to the underside of a helicopter landing pad, which is elevated above the roof. Architect Morgan calls these courts "inverted pyramids of space" in reference to his interests in the ancient architecture of the local Indians. As the development of downtown Jacksonville moves in its direction, the roof-top park (photo left) will gain increasing importance as both open space and as a place for people to relax. Consistent with his interests in urban context, the preservation of a nineteenth century firehouse on the site was successfully urged by Morgan, and the building has been converted to a museum for historic fire-fighting equipment (photo bottom).

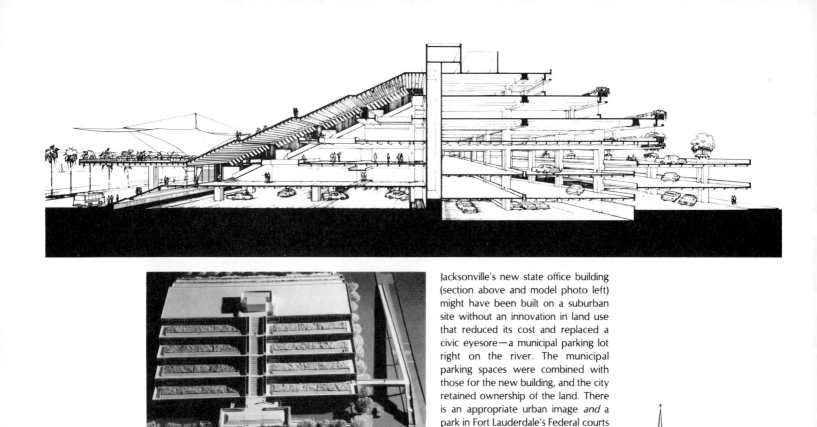

Jacksonville's new state office building (section above and model photo left) might have been built on a suburban site without an innovation in land use that reduced its cost and replaced a civic eyesore—a municipal parking lot right on the river. The municipal parking spaces were combined with those for the new building, and the city retained ownership of the land. There is an appropriate urban image *and* a park in Fort Lauderdale's Federal courts building (drawing below).

Similar thoughtful approaches in Morgan's design are seen in a comparison of the police headquarters to two other civic buildings. They are a Florida State office building in Jacksonville (model photo and section top), and a Federal courts building in Fort Lauderdale (drawing above). The office building is conceived as a ceremonial viewing platform with roof-top terraces that step down to the adjacent river. Here, Morgan was instrumental in having the building on a downtown site by promoting an arrangement whereby the State could rent land over a municipal parking lot, and incorporate the former use in the new structure. The courts building makes an appropriately strong urban statement, while providing a public-related park within the building's over-all framework.

These two buildings share with the Police Memorial Building several other of Morgan's concepts besides the innovative use of their sites. Most obvious are forms generated by Morgan's interest in what he is currently researching—local indigenous Indian architecture, which Morgan expects to demonstrate as rivaling that of the Aztecs and Mayans. Ceremonial forms, such as great earth pyramids and processional routes, sunken below the ground, were important elements of that architecture.

Partially because of such interests in historical monumentality and partially as an innovative way to reduce floor-to-floor heights, Morgan—along with engineers William Le Messurier and William Lam—developed a system of structural precast-concrete "trees" for the police building. (The concept was later carried over to the courts building.) In the system, each column supports two cantilevered beams at right angles. The beams in turn support edge beams that define a section of the structure, which is only tied to the next "tree" by a flat concrete slab over the intervening space. Under the flat slabs, the intersecting beam-free areas can accommodate the horizontal mechanical and electrical services, as can be seen in the photos on pages 67–69, and in the drawing of the courts building above.

Considering the innovation and amenity in these buildings, it is interesting to discover that there has been a tight control of costs. The police station was completed early in 1978 for just over $40 per square foot, on a fast-track schedule that required eight separate construction contracts. The State office building's basic contract was twenty-five per cent under budget.

POLICE MEMORIAL BUILDING, Jacksonville, Florida. Architects: *William Morgan Architects—associate-in-charge: Thomas McCrary*. Engineers: *William Le Messurier* (structural theory); *H.W. Keister & Associates* (applied structural); *Haley Keister & Associates* (foundation and soils); *Roy Turknett Engineers* (mechanical/electrical). Consultants: *William Lam Associates* (lighting); *Ed Heist, Jr.* (interiors); *Hilton Meadows* (landscape); *Meyer/Lomprey & Associates* (graphics). General contractor: *Orr Construction Company*.

114th PRECINCT STATION

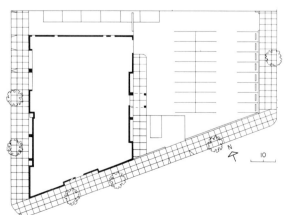

This building, a well studied design in the classic manner of the New Brutalism of the late 40's and 50's, makes a dignified appearance in a haphazard environment along a freeway in Queens, New York (photo above right), and adapts itself without rancor to the residential scale of the adjacent side streets (photos right). It is a police station which houses district as well as precinct level functions on a trapezoidal lot (site plan left). Placing the building on the street line gave a maximum area for police parking and for the temporary storage of abandoned vehicles. The building itself and the low wall that surrounds the parking lot occupy the entire site, thus providing both security and screening for the parking area, and maintain-

John Yang

ing the traditional format of this residential area—street, sidewalk and building.

The exterior walls are brick and concrete; security windows and the entrances are of black anodized aluminum. All of the materials were chosen for their durability, their economy and their promise of lasting good appearance. The demarkation between the floors is emphasized by the recessed edge of the floor slab.

114th PRECINCT STATION, Queens, New York. Architects: *Holden/Yang/Raemsch/Terjesen—partner-in-charge, John Yang; project architect, James D. Crabb.* Engineers: *Throop & Feiden* (structural); *Kallen & Lamelson* (mechanical/electrical). Consultant: *H. A. Sloane Associates* (cost). General contractor: *Renel Construction Incorporated.*

FEDERAL CORRECTIONAL FACILITY BUTNER, NORTH CAROLINA

This medium- to high-security Federal correctional institution was originally conceived as a service facility to house mentally disturbed and otherwise abnormal inmates from other Federal prisons in the East. The goal was to design a complex that was more "humane" than prisons normally are—with less visible security systems, fewer inmates, and an over-all look that was not institutional or oppressive. To those ends, the traditional gun tower was eliminated, and only an irregularly octagonal double fence defines the outer perimeter. Three clusters of housing units designed for mentally ill inmates are located together on one part of the site (see model photo opposite), and most of the rest of the buildings help enclose an outdoor space that is thought of as a kind of village green. With this "cottage-like" arrangement of buildings, though, adequate care was taken to make for adequate visual control of inmates by a minimum number of staff. The photo above shows the chapel and auditorium building in the center of the green.

FEDERAL CORRECTIONAL INSTITUTION, Butner, North Carolina. Owner: *United States Department of Justice, Bureau of Prisons.* Architects: *Middleton, McMillan, Architects, Inc.—project designer: Ronald W. Touchstone.* Engineers: *Frank B. Hicks Associates* (structural); *Mechanical Engineers, Inc.* (mechanical); *John Bolen Engineers* (electrical). General contractor: *G. C. Tandy Construction Co.*

FOLEY SQUARE COURTHOUSE ANNEX: ATTORNEYS' OFFICE AND METROPOLITAN CORRECTIONAL CENTER NEW YORK CITY

Located near the Police Headquarters Building, seen earlier in this chapter, this project represents a major effort to create a humane prison environment. The architects concentrated on reducing negative stresses associated with incarceration by creating a ''normative'' environment, according to architect Paul Silver, that gives a freedom of movement to the prisoner within an obviously limited area. To achieve this, the design included providing large open interior spaces, with extensive number of windows, decentralized dining areas, acoustical control to minimize noise, and a visually inconspicuous security system. Every detail was studied, including specifying non-traditional hardware.

FOLEY SQUARE COURTHOUSE ANNEX: THE OFFICE BUILDING FOR THE U.S. ATTORNEYS AND THE METROPOLITAN CORRECTIONAL CENTER, New York, New York. Owner: *General Services Administration, U.S. Department of Justice.* Architect: *Gruzen & Partners—Jordan Gruzen and Peter Samton, partners-in-charge of planning and design; Lloyd Fleischman, project director; Paul Silver, director of justice facilities; Gordon Vance, project manager; Robert Genchek, principal designer.* Engineers: *Strobel Associates (structural); Cosentini Associates (mechanical).* Landscape architects: *M. Paul Friedberg & Associates.* Food service consultants: *Romano & Associates.* General contractor: *Castagna & Sons.*

David Hirsch photos except as noted

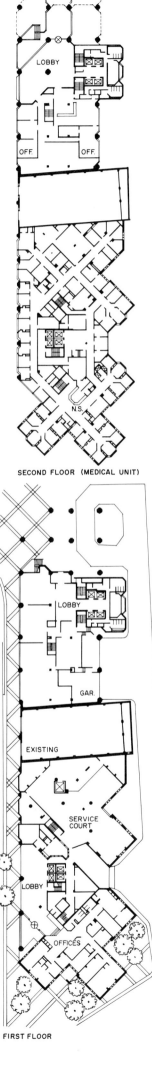

SECOND FLOOR (MEDICAL UNIT)

FIRST FLOOR

Hirsch/Fine

Nathaniel Lieberman

WASHTENAW COUNTY CORRECTIONS/LAW ENFORCEMENT CENTER, ANN ARBOR, MICHIGAN

This facility is designed for a predominantly pre-trial population, but with some facilities for sentenced offenders. Housing 239 men and women, it is located on a 39-acre site bounded on one side by houses in the $100,000 range and on the other by a major apartment complex. The architects therefore were very sensitive to height limitations, to creating a scale throughout that was compatible with the neighbors, and to providing the ample court-required outdoor exercise spaces with internal courtyards (see drawing, right) rather than a more spread-out campus scheme that a site of this size might have suggested.

The County Law Enforcement Center is located close to the road, convenient to public parking and visually related to other County buildings on the site. A service yard serves as a buffer between this public area and the security areas. Adjoining the service yard is a building element containing admissions, processing and booking functions, and such central support facilities as library, classrooms, offices, the gymnasium, staff dining room, and clinics. Inmate housing units, enclosing outdoor exercise courtyards, are located on a series of terraces running down the sloping site. The outer wall of the housing units functions as the security perimeter, minimizing fences or walls.

Housing units are divided into living units

Balthazar Korab photos except as noted

Barbara Elliott Martin

of 16 single-occupancy rooms grouped around a split-level living room—and meals, library service are delivered to these shared spaces. Two housing units—or clusters of 32 inmates—share a common day room opening to an outdoor court.

WASHTENAW COUNTY CORRECTIONS/LAW EN-FORCEMENT CENTER, Ann Arbor, Michigan. Architects: *Hellmuth, Obata & Kassabaum; Colvin-Robinson Associates, Inc., associated architects.* Engineers: *Jack D. Gillum & Associates, Ltd (structural); Ayres & Hayakawa (mechanical/electrical).* Civil engineer/landscape architect/interior design: *Hellmuth, Obata & Kassabaum.* General contractor: *Spence Brothers.*

LEXINGTON ASSESSMENT AND RECEPTION FACILITY, LEXINGTON, OKLAHOMA

As the latest development at this regional correction center (which serves many counties in central Oklahoma), the housing units were designed as a prototype for the state's correctional system. This facility houses 240 inmates who are serving both short- and long-term sentences.

In appearance, the project is residential in scale and character. Each housing unit is comprised of two modules, linked to a separate education/vocational building which also contains the unit manager's office. Each unit houses 80 persons, but each prisoner has a private cell. The rooms are clustered in groups of 20 around a split-level day room. A central control room for each module provides electronic monitoring of all doors and entrances.

One housing unit is set off from the other two for persons requiring special supervision, and can be isolated if necessary. Between this housing and the other units are common facilities of gymnasium, library, chapel, and dining hall.

LEXINGTON ASSESSMENT AND RECEPTION FACILITY, PHASE II, Lexington, Oklahoma. Architects: *Benham-Blair & Affiliates, Inc. and Hellmuth, Obata & Kassabaum.* Engineers: *Benham-Blair & Affiliates, Inc. (structural/mechanical); Hayakawa Associates (electrical).* General contractor: *Harmon Construction Company.*

Kiku Obata photos

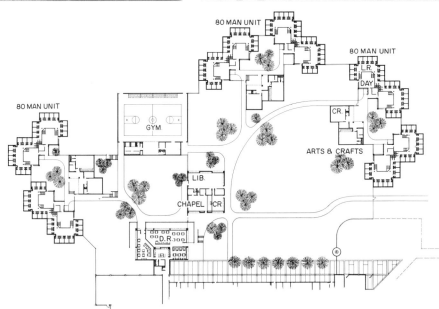

MENDOCINO COUNTY DETENTION CENTER AND JUSTICE COURT UKIAH, CALIFORNIA

This facility for sentenced misdemeanants is located on a highly unusual site—near a prominent residential area. The design, therefore, is highly responsive to the community.

Four buildings form a pleasant mini-campus for both male and female inmates in a primarily minimum-security system (although there is an area designated for medium security). The men are housed in two residential buildings and the women are located in a building which also provides housing for men awaiting trial and administrative offices, infirmary and visiting rooms. The fourth building in the complex is for recreation and dining.

As a minimum-security complex, the cells are located along the perimeter, which is lined with windows. These cells surround an open area which leads to a central day room (along with laundry and counseling facilities).

In an effort to blend the buildings with the site and increase its acceptance by the neighborhood community, the design was kept simple, with appropriate scale and massing of the buildings, a wood exterior and covered walkways.

MENDOCINO COUNTY DETENTION CENTER AND JUSTICE COURT, Ukiah, California. Architect: *Kaplan-McLaughlin*. Engineers: *Anderson & Culley (structural); JYA Design Associates (mechanical); The Engineering Enterprise (electrical).* General contractor: *Todd Construction Company.*

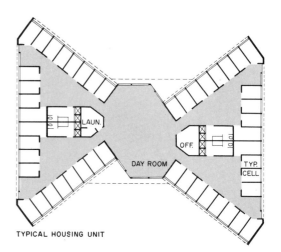

TYPICAL HOUSING UNIT

LAUN.

OFF.

DAY ROOM

TYP. CELL

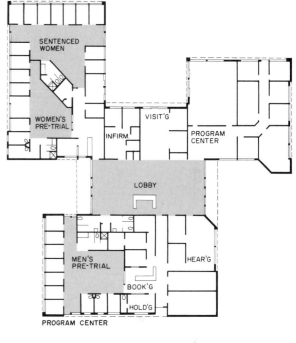

SENTENCED WOMEN

WOMEN'S PRE-TRIAL

INFIRM.

VISIT'G

PROGRAM CENTER

LOBBY

MEN'S PRE-TRIAL

HEAR'G

BOOK'G

HOLD'G

PROGRAM CENTER

WAREHOUSE

LIBRARY

ST.

KIT.

LAUN.

DINING

BARBER

COMMUNITY CENTER

RAMSEY COUNTY DETENTION CENTER, ST. PAUL, MINNESOTA

This facility is designed to house 150 inmates in a cliff-side facility overlooking the Mississippi River. It is intended only for short-term detention—average stays are 1½ days for misdemeanants and 10 days for félons. This short-term imprisonment played an important part in the design concept: it suggested that the facility should be subdivided, under a unit-management concept, into 16-room housing units, each with a day room and dining space. Each unit is 4,000 square feet in area. There is adequate space for games and exercise equipment in each unit, but there is no large indoor or outdoor recreation area.

Says Paul Silver of Gruzen and Partners: "Here, more than in any other facility we

have done, the restrictedness of the living area raises important concerns. A unit of 16 rooms produces a relatively small total group living area. Doubling the unit size to 32 rooms would have produced twice the available free area, and possibly altered the 'compressiveness' of the environment; yet this would have made security more difficult and probably required mixing inmates detained for minor and more serious crimes—which is not desirable programmatically. The question remains: is 4,000 square feet enough space to house 16 people for two weeks (or perhaps more time for some) without negative depressive effects that could lead to extreme behavior? We really do not know."

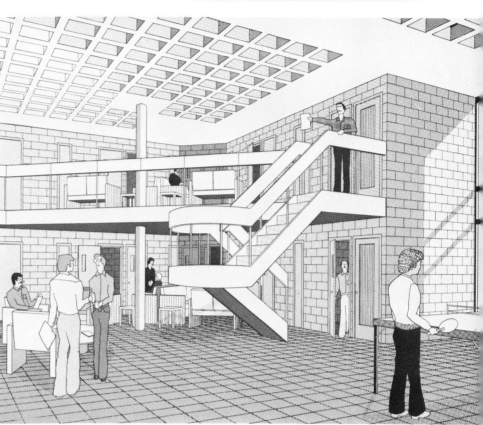

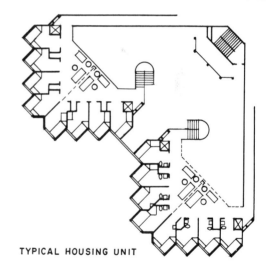

TYPICAL HOUSING UNIT

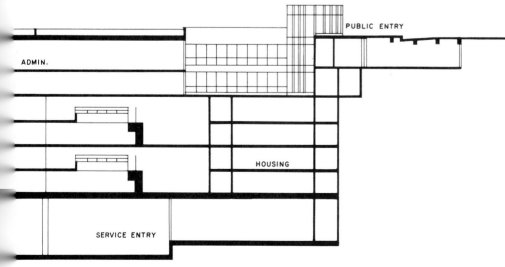

The park on top of the facility (drawing above) is a public facility—an amenity that helped reduce neighborhood reluctance in accepting the facility.

RAMSEY COUNTY ADULT DETENTION CENTER, St. Paul, Minnesota. Owner: *Ramsey County.* Architects: *The Wold Association—Fred J. Shank, principal in charge; Clarke D. Wold, project coordinator; Raymond A. Keller, project architect.* Associated architects: *Gruzen & Partners—Peter Samton, director of design; Paul Silver, director justice facilities; Virendra Girdhar, principal designer.* Consulting engineers: *Kirkham Michael Associates.* Food service consultant: *Van Hemerd Associates.* General contractor: *Steenberg Construction Co.*

Englewood, New Jersey's new public works
facility is an almost monumental building
for very mundane functions

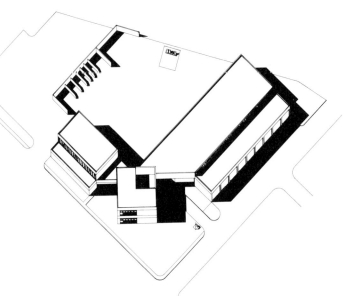

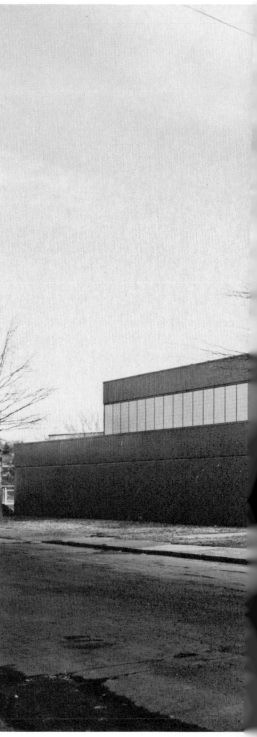

Designed to house and service vehicles, architect James Polshek and Associates' new facility is divided into a repair shop (left in isometric) and a large garage, with a two-story office structure in between. Lacking adjacent buildings with which to relate, the building forms a strong sculptural composition with the most ordinary of materials. On a steel structure, bright red steel-faced asbestos wall panels are integrated into a proprietary aluminum curtain-wall system. The aluminum system integrates windows, translucent clerestories in the garage areas, and even the bright blue garage doors. The angled building forms two sides of a court of almost ceremonial proportions where vehicles are parked. The building and walls screen vehicles from the streets and adjacent properties. The office building contains facilities for operations personnel on the ground floor, and administration offices on the second floor.

DEPARTMENT OF PUBLIC WORKS FACILITY, Englewood, New Jersey. Owner: *City of Englewood.* Architects: *James Stewart Polshek and Associates—associate in charge: Dimitri Linard; job captain: Howard Sussel.* Engineers: *Pfister, Tor and Associates (structural); Bornikel Engineering (mechanical/electrical).* Consultant: *William Baum, Inc (costs).* General contractor: *Sullivan Magee Sullivan.*

CHAPTER THREE

BUILDINGS AND FACILITIES FOR PARKS AND RECREATION: PAVILIONS, LODGES, YOUTH CENTERS AND STADIA

Ten years ago, California's director of the State Department of Parks and Recreation, William Penn Mott, Jr., noted that 40 million people had used the State's parks in one year, and he and his staff were in the process of gearing up for the deluge to come. Mott and the directors of the other states' parks and recreational facilities have not been disappointed, for the deluge has surely come. But it could be wished that all of the states' directors had had Mott's foresight in recognizing the potential problems. As Mott's particular mandate was outdoor recreation, he and the Department had produced a computerized model of the use for which each state park was best suited—preservation, recreation or somewhere in between—down to knowing the numbers and kinds of users that could be accommodated on a daily basis. By means of this management tool the system could be efficient.

On the following pages are a number of different parks and recreational facilities. Not all are in California, nor are they part of a grand plan. The facilities are simply well done, and they meet a number of public recreational needs. As this book's preface explained, they can be youth centers for "underprivileged" fledglings in an urban ghetto or for an "overprivileged" group in a Miami suburb. The point—of course—is that they fit the needs of the real users, which—again of course—is the real role of governments' involvement in the whole area, whether or not the physical result lies within an overall masterplan.

Accordingly, the reader will see here everything from the ghetto youth center to the Miami product mentioned above. He or she will see a lodge designed for only those with their own airplanes, and country camps designed so that urban youths can see the other side of mainstreet.

But every example illustrates the true message of this booklet—that buildings and facilities can be designed as best befits their use, their circumstances and their architects' desires to produce a good product. And the diversity of these facilities recognizes the expanded role of government, not only in providing such facilities in the first place, but also in recognizing the increasing complications of the very nature of their use.

Airpark Lodge at Reelfoot Lake

The master plan for development of Reelfoot Lake State Park recognized the great fragility of this swampy wilderness lake and the importance of preserving it undisturbed, and it set up a number of basic design premises for implementation of the plan. When the architects for the master plan were commissioned to design the first phase of the development, it was this aspect—the relating of the project to the natural surroundings, with minimal disturbance to the flora and fauna of the area—that they found to be the most challenging part of the job. That they were successful is obvious.

Reelfoot Lake was formed in 1811–12 as a result of the great New Madrid Earthquake which caused the Mississippi River to flood extensively on either side of its channel. After the river resumed its natural course, what had been a vast sunken cypress forest remained flooded, and became Reelfoot Lake. Located in the northwest corner of Tennessee, the Lake has an area of some 18,000 acres at normal level. Although it has been for many years a paradise for hunters and fishermen, much of it is still wilderness. Making it possible for many people to enjoy the very special beauty of this unique place was the goal of the state's master plan. Airpark Lodge—so called from the existing airstrip for fly-in campers—and the development around it is the first step toward the implementing of this goal.

The swampy nature of the site made the use of piers particularly appropriate, since they could extend through the swamp without disturbing either trees or water plants and would allow the development to spread out, minimizing its impact and at the same time maximizing the visitor's experience of the place.

The Lodge complex consists of several buildings set on pilings over the water and connected to the main pier by short walks. At the entrance to the pier is the park office with a supply shop and a boat rental dock adjacent. Beyond the office, astride the pier, is the restaurant/lounge building with decks for outdoor dining, and farther along are clusters of motel units among the trees, each of the 20 units with a balcony for fishing or for looking at this almost-wilderness. At the lake end of the 600-foot pier is a public fishing deck. The interiors and the engaging graphics, bold against simple rough sawn cypress board, were designed by the architects.

AIRPARK LODGE, REELFOOT LAKE STATE PARK, Tiptonville, Tennessee. Architects: *Gassner/Nathan/Browne.* Engineers: *Wooten, Smith & Weiss* (structural); *Pickering Engineering* (foundation, soils, mechanical/electrical). General contractor: *McAdoo Contractors, Inc.*

Otto Baitz photos

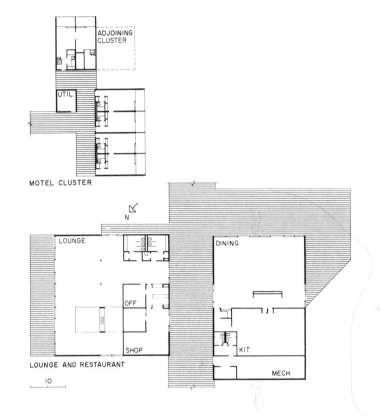

ADJOINING
CLUSTER

UTIL

MOTEL CLUSTER

N

LOUNGE

DINING

OFF

SHOP

KIT.

MECH.

LOUNGE AND RESTAURANT

10

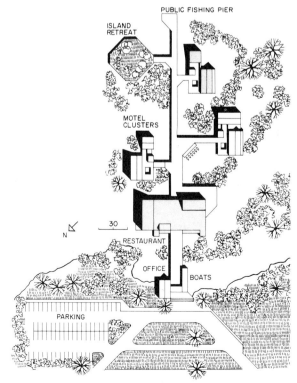

PUBLIC FISHING PIER

ISLAND
RETREAT

MOTEL
CLUSTERS

N   30

RESTAURANT

OFFICE

BOATS

PARKING

John McNanie

SAINT PETERS PARK RECREATION CENTER PROVIDES FOR ACTIVE PURSUITS

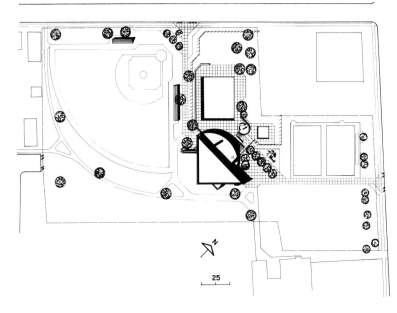

Interjecting facilities for the kind of lively involvement that keeps neighborhood youngsters alert and interested, this airy pavilion and large swimming pool occupy part of a more traditional park that once primarily catered to the sedate habits of strolling and sitting. The pavilion houses changing rooms and machinery for the pool—as well as offices and a large multiple-use space, overlooked by a balcony snack bar (see plans overleaf). The balcony extends out of the building to a large semi-circular terrace, where ventilation stacks from the changing rooms below have been bent into playful white sculptures.

The arrangement allows quieter pursuits at the second level, out of the heavy traffic to and from the changing rooms. A ramp to the second level projects from the building, and allows access for the handicapped. The long diagonal wall facing the pool is glazed with unusually large sheets of clear shatterproof plastic, allowing both views toward the pool and surveillance of indoor activities from two of the adjacent streets. The other two walls of brick are almost solid, shielding the sun from the south and supporting two sides of the steel roof structure.

After two years' use, the $1.1-million facility remains almost as fresh and spotless as the day it opened, in a neighborhood where graffiti and vandalism are common. The architects attribute a large part

Nathaniel Lieberman

Nathaniel Lieberman

of this success to the sense of possession and pride that the users have in this new neighborhood focus. Accordingly, this project provides them with one of their greater sources of satisfaction and pleasure. It is also proof of their feeling about the importance of really getting to know the particular neighborhood in which a project is to be built—a crucial element in their design process.

In keeping with these particular architects' highly pragmatic design approach, Saint Peters is an interesting mix of practicality and playfulness. The combination of the triangle and the semicircular forms grew as much from a desire to reinforce natural circulation patterns and to create a meaningful relationship between pool and building, as it did from a desire for a fresh image. Similarly, the two-levels were the result of the need for a separation of different types of activities. And they were the result of a desire for interesting spatial relationships.

SAINT PETERS PARK RECREATION CENTER, Newark, New Jersey. Owner: *City of Newark*. Architects: *Ciardullo Ehmann—project architect: Paul Spears*. Engineers: *Environmental Engineering (soils); George Deng (air handling); Marian Swiechowski (plumbing, electrical, swimming pool)*. Landscape architect: *Miceli Weed Kulik*. Cost consultant: *Thomas Barrella*. General contractor: *Guasto Construction*.

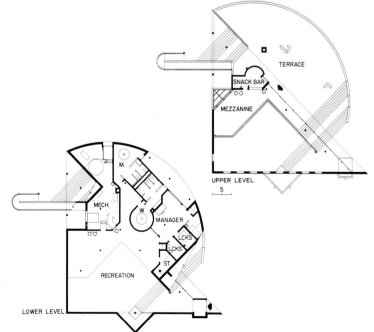

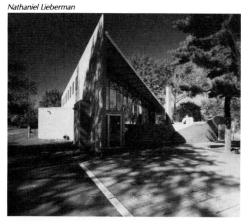

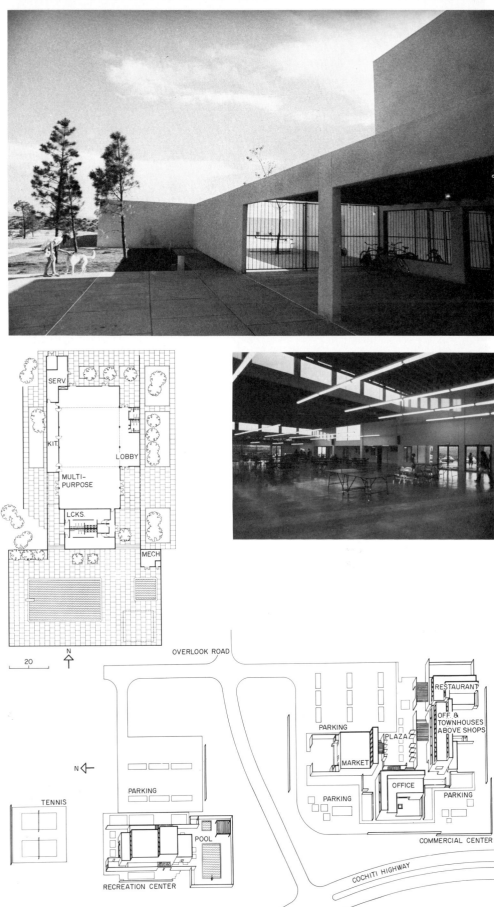

Cochiti Lake Recreation Center

Cochiti is a new town being developed in the high desert country north of Albuquerque, New Mexico, on an Indian reservation. To serve both the new residents and the long-time pueblo residents, a Town Center with shops, offices, restaurant, crafts studios and apartments, is being built.

Cochiti Lake Recreation Center is the first building to be completed in the Center. It provides for both indoor activities and outdoor sports—its indoor facilities including a large game and assembly room which can be divided into smaller spaces, a kitchen, offices, and locker rooms to serve the two outdoor pools and two tennis courts.

This first building of the Center has been designed with the harsh character of the surrounding countryside as the determinant. The climate is hot, dry and windy, the earth dusty, vegetation sparse, and relief from the heat is welcome. The architectural solution derives from the intent to provide a building which would "temper the formidable elements of the place and employ its more amiable features. It was, accordingly, designed to be a hospitable, inviting place which pueblo children and Cochiti residents can adapt to their wishes." Thus, on the south and west there are no windows; light comes from the north and east, and even from these sources is controlled. Clerestory windows in step-backed walls admit an even amount of light to the assembly room at all times. Entrances are sheltered from direct sun and from winds.

Despite its harsh qualities, the setting for this building is spectacular, with mountains rising behind it, open sky above it and, as yet, nothing to disturb the great openness around it. The form of the building is simple but bold, horizontal planes responding to the land, the high central element reminiscent of Southwestern mesas. The exterior walls are a cool sky blue in color, physically and psychologically effective, as they reflect the sun's intense heat and also at the same time suggest coolness. The stucco is rough textured, and wood where used and exposed, is rough sawn—appropriate to the simple details designed to make the building's execution, under less then usual conditions, feasible. The building was completed in December 1973.

COCHITI LAKE RECREATION CENTER, Cochiti, New Mexico. Architects: *Frank O. Gehry and Associates.* Engineers: *Joseph Kinoshita & Associates* (structural). Landscape architects: *Sasaki Walker & Associates, Inc.* Contractor: *Great Western Cities Corporation, Inc.*

1. Future camp
2. Picnic area
3. Camp circle
4. Bus parking
5. Future model farm
6. Pond
7. Ski and sled run
8. Nature trail
9. Natural amphitheater
10. Open for vista
11. Knoll

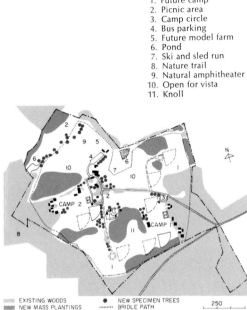

EXISTING WOODS   ● NEW SPECIMEN TREES
NEW MASS PLANTINGS   ····· BRIDLE PATH   250

MILLDALE CAMPS

Reisterstown, Maryland
RTKL, Inc.

The Milldale Camps of the Jewish Community Center are located on a 155-acre site northwest of Baltimore, and serve a variety of purposes: city children get a taste of the country, adults and families use the camps year round for weekend outings and older people use an old farmhouse (existing on the property) for their activities. The site is kept as natural as possible, with the buildings—simple and modest wood structures with steep hipped roofs—unassertedly placed on the hillside, with the knoll kept open. Each of the basic units is 20 feet square; some with open, railed sides are used for shelters; others with red cedar walls are utility buildings. There are 20 such structures in each camp, and the camps, on the edge of the forest around the open hill, are almost concealed in spring and summer when the trees are in leaf. Each camp also has a large open pavilion located up the slope. In the open meadow are two swimming pools with minimal dressing shelters. Camps are far enough apart for their programs, simultaneously involving some 1000 young people, to be under way simultaneously without conflict.

MILLDALE CAMPS, Reisterstown, Maryland. Owner: *Jewish Community Center of Baltimore*. Architects: *RTKL Inc.—Charles E. Lamb, partner-in-charge; Paul T. Heineman, project captain*. Contractor: *Ira C. Rigger, Inc.*

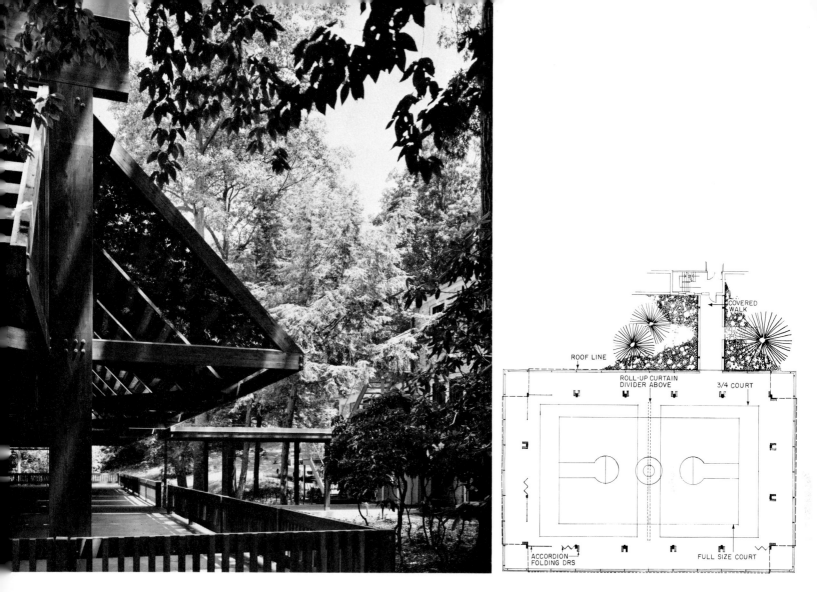

Joseph W. Molitor Photos

ALL-WEATHER PAVILION FOR ALL KINDS OF PLAY

Open but protected, this 10,000 square foot play area—designed for a school but suitable for outdoor recreation of many kinds in a variety of locations—is used for outdoor games and other activities all year round, regardless of weather. On very cold days, radiant heat in the ceiling can be used and on windy days, canvas drops can be lowered along the perimeter to form walls. Fixed glass triangle at the corners give additional protection. The louvered wood overhangs shed rain and snow while admitting ample air. So pleasant is the "gymkhana" (Hindu for sports arena) that adults of the community use it after hours for their activities. The structure is simple but handled with skill and a sure eye for proportion, line, and the quality of space created. Twenty laminated wood girders 60 feet long by three feet deep span the court area and carry the roof, and are supported by 20-foot high columns which rest on a concrete slab.

GYMKHANA, ELISABETH MORROW SCHOOL, Englewood, New Jersey, Architect: *Delnoce Whitney Goubert*; structural engineers: *Fraioli, Blum & Yesselman*; landscape designer: *Thomas F. Paterson*; contractor: *Romangino Construction Company.*

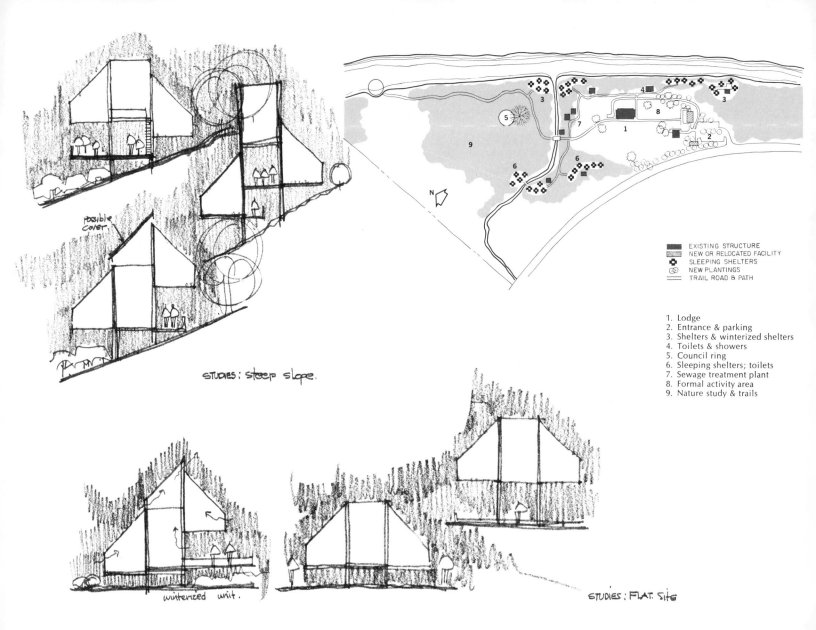

STUDIES: steep slope.

winterized unit.

STUDIES: FLAT Site

EXISTING STRUCTURE
NEW OR RELOCATED FACILITY
SLEEPING SHELTERS
NEW PLANTINGS
TRAIL ROAD & PATH

1. Lodge
2. Entrance & parking
3. Shelters & winterized shelters
4. Toilets & showers
5. Council ring
6. Sleeping shelters; toilets
7. Sewage treatment plant
8. Formal activity area
9. Nature study & trails

Robert Lindsay photos

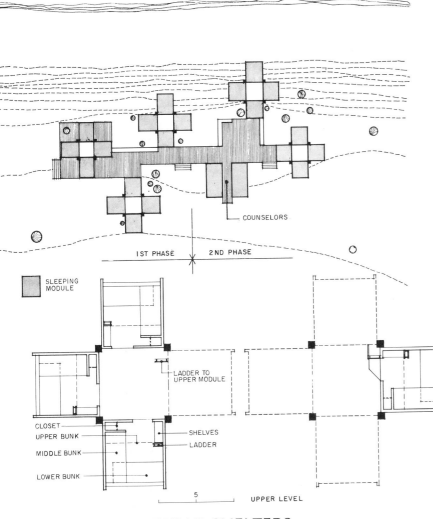

SIUSLAW RIVER

COUNSELORS

1ST PHASE — 2ND PHASE

SLEEPING MODULE

LADDER TO UPPER MODULE

CLOSET
UPPER BUNK — SHELVES
MIDDLE BUNK — LADDER
LOWER BUNK

5   UPPER LEVEL

UPRIGHT 2 x 6'S WINTER UNIT ONLY

CAMP LANE SLEEPING SHELTERS

Mapleton, Oregon
Unthank Seder and Poticha

County owned and administered, Camp Lane is used by organizations for conferences, programs and camping, with especial emphasis on young people's and children's groups. The architects were asked to prepare a master site plan to incorporate new shelters (some winterized) into an existing camp, for an eventual 150 persons. The 15-acre site is small for such a density; shelters are located on the edge of open activity spaces. Decks and elevated areas double as conference and play areas. Each unit is self-contained: furnishings are built in, simple and rugged. Because the camp is in such constant use, new construction has to be done fast and in brief periods. A prefabricated panel system permits rapid erection: a basic unit can be erected in slightly less than an hour, a group of 12 finished in one month. Units are grouped in clusters of four, with three persons to a unit. More units will be added as budget permits. The forms, bright colors, siting among trees, and interplay of decks were designed to be "different from home" and "fun" for all users, but particularly for children.

SLEEPING SHELTERS, CAMP LANE, (Phases 1 & 2), near Mapleton, Oregon. Architects: *Unthank, Seder & Poticha.* Contractor: *Lane County Parks Department (Phase I), Howard Nelson (Phase II).*

DRAKE'S BEACH FACILITIES BUILDING

Point Reyes National Seashore, California
Worley K. Wong, John Carden Campbell

This visitor facilities building is the first such to be built in the new Point Reyes National Seashore, some 30 miles northwest of San Francisco, for which funds were authorized to complete acquisition of private lands within its overall boundaries. The building, housing ranger's office, dressing rooms, garage and dining facilities, is for year-round use, in weather which varies from dense fog to warm bright sun, with winds which range from light to uncomfortably strong. The four uses of the building determined the plan and provided the desirable addition of a protected court for wind-free lounging and for interpretive talks by rangers. The slant of the roofs aids in reducing the amount of wind that reaches the court. The building is of wood construction, and stands on piles 30 and 40 feet long. Pilings are used throughout the building itself, treated with weathering oil. Like the other materials used, including the copper roof, they were selected because they required minimum maintenance.

DRAKE'S BEACH FACILITIES BUILDING, Point Reyes National Seashore, California. Architects: *Worley K. Wong* of *Wong & Brocchini & Associates* and *John Carden Campbell* of *Campbell & Rocchia & Associates*. Structural engineers: *Eric Elsesser & Associates*.

Joshua Freiwald photos

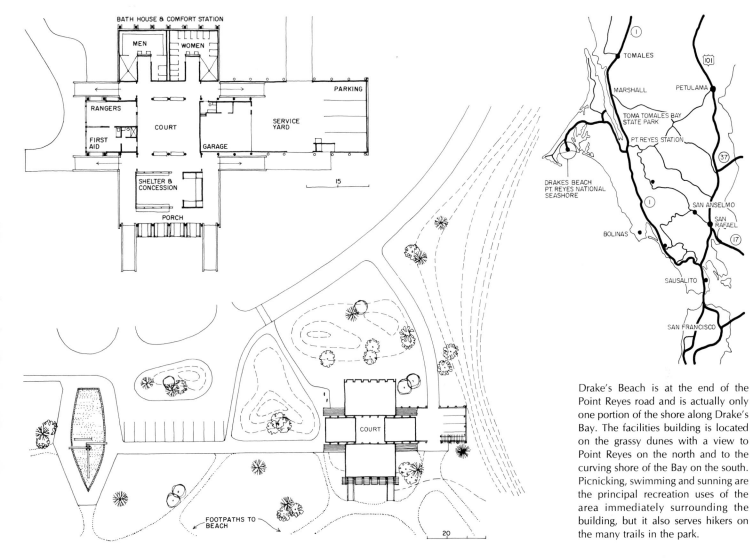

Drake's Beach is at the end of the Point Reyes road and is actually only one portion of the shore along Drake's Bay. The facilities building is located on the grassy dunes with a view to Point Reyes on the north and to the curving shore of the Bay on the south. Picnicking, swimming and sunning are the principal recreation uses of the area immediately surrounding the building, but it also serves hikers on the many trails in the park.

INWOOD HILL PARK NATURE TRAILS

New York City
Richard G. Stein and Associates

Walking for pleasure is—and will be, say recreation experts—one of this country's most popular recreation activities. But pleasant places to walk are few in number, especially in urban areas. The new nature trails at Inwood Hill Park are rare exceptions to the insensitivity of walks in city parks. This old park—a unique remnant of Manhattan's original natural state, historic in connotation, wild in much of its extensive acreage—is surrounded by the densely populated streets of New York City, and is easily accessible to city dwellers. The three new trails have been developed with exceptional sensitivity to the natural qualities of these environments. Restraint and subtlety of design keep man-made intrusion at a minimum but at the same time introduce new ways of heightening the outdoor experience: the concrete "information prism" with rocks and plant materials cast into its acrylic plastic top; sitting terraces and resting places using simple forms in informal groupings.

INWOOD HILL PARK NATURE TRAILS, New York City. Client: *New York City Parks, Recreation and Cultural Affairs Administration—August Heckscher, Administrator; Elliot Willensky, Deputy Administrator for Development; Roy Neuberger, Director of Conservation.* Architects: *Richard G. Stein & Associates—Diane Serber, associate-in-charge.* Contractor: *Whitler Construction Company.*

Many new plantings were specified along the trails: on River Cove, blueberry, bayberry, mountain laurel and hemlock; on Rock Face, ferns, iris, narcissus, dogwoods; on Woodland Summit, flowering trees, hyacinths, mountain laurel, narcissus, daffodils, viburnum. Plant materials were selected (with suggestions from City horticulturists) to enhance existing plant materials with seasonal color and variations of texture.

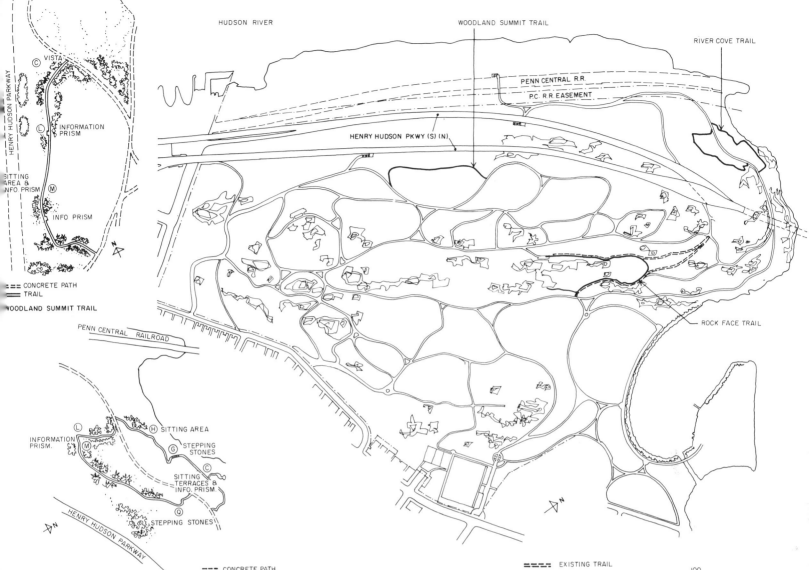

HUDSON RIVER

WOODLAND SUMMIT TRAIL

RIVER COVE TRAIL

PENN CENTRAL R.R.

P.C. R.R. EASEMENT

HENRY HUDSON PKWY (S) (N)

ROCK FACE TRAIL

C VISTA

L INFORMATION PRISM

SITTING AREA & INFO. PRISM

M INFO PRISM

HENRY HUDSON PARKWAY

=== CONCRETE PATH
— TRAIL

WOODLAND SUMMIT TRAIL

PENN CENTRAL RAILROAD

L
M INFORMATION PRISM.

H SITTING AREA

G STEPPING STONES

C SITTING TERRACES & INFO. PRISM.

Q STEPPING STONES

HENRY HUDSON PARKWAY

RIVER COVE TRAIL

=== CONCRETE PATH
— TRAIL

==== EXISTING TRAIL
—— NEW OR REHABILITATED TRAIL

100

Red Maple

Acer rubrum

Diane Serber photos

103

TENT PAVILION FOR FLOWER SHOW AT STATE FAIR

Philip L. Molten photos

Fairs are major, though often brief, recreational opportunities, usually housed in undistinguished, utilitarian structures. California's new State Exposition and Fair, however, capitalizing on a mild climate and a large population to draw attendance, was designed to provide for year-round operation, with exhibits and expositions housed in buildings designed by some of the state's best-known architects. The unusual Floriculture Pavilion, part of the Fair Activities Complex, is a favorite place for fairgoers, an oasis of color and greenery under a ceiling of filtered light, where visitors can stroll, picnic or sit and talk. The structure is steel cable with canvas panels and flies which can be removed completely or partially to obtain different effects. A double flap system of panels on the sides creates patterns of light and shadow on tent walls both inside and outside. A waterway meanders through the display area and connects with the lake.

FLORICULTURE PAVILION, FAIR ACTIVITIES COMPLEX, California State Exposition and Fair, Sacramento, California. Architects: coordinating and master plan, *Wurster, Bernardi & Emmons;* pavilion, *Callister and Payne;* structural engineers: *Gilbert Forsberg Diekmann & Schmidt;* mechanical engineer: *Paul Rosenthal;* electrical engineers: *Charles Krieger & Associates;* landscape architects: *Lawrence Halprin & Associates;* contractor: *Baldwin Contracting Co.* (complex), *Industrial Covers* (pavilion).

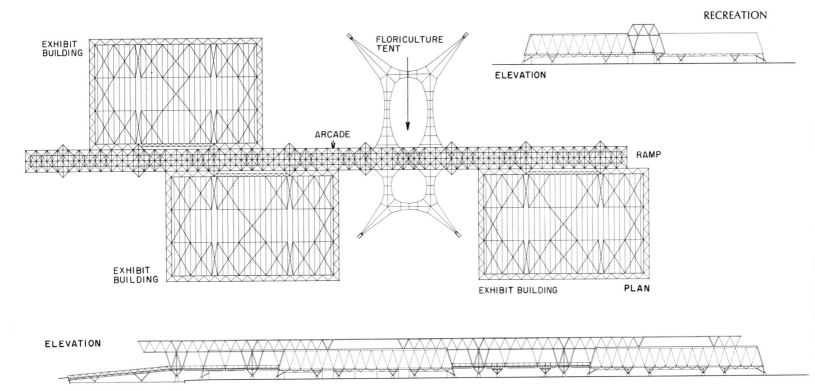

EXHIBIT BUILDING

FLORICULTURE TENT

RECREATION

ELEVATION

ARCADE

RAMP

EXHIBIT BUILDING

EXHIBIT BUILDING

PLAN

ELEVATION

The dramatic entrance to the Fair Activities Complex was designed to be a steel-framed covered walkway which bridges the floriculture tent and connects the central Fair plaza with the livestock and grandstand area some distance away, permitting visitors to see a wide variety of exhibits on their way. Stairs lead from this bridge and its mezzanine exhibit areas to the lower level where there is direct access to the tent. Exhibit buildings are steel framed, their exposed trusses providing a vast clear space where the traditional state fair exhibits are displayed. Other recreation encludes boating on the lake in front of the complex and "water rides" through the tent.

COAL STREET POOL

Coal Street Park derives its name from a former colliery on the 36-acre site which once separated two economically diverse neighborhoods and is now intended to become a meeting ground of recreational activities. The project was backed by the State Department of Community Affairs, the Federal Model Cities Program, other Federal agencies, and the owners, the City of Wilkes-Barre, Pennsylvania. The latter commissioned The Allen Organization as park and recreational planners, who in turn hired the firm of Bohlin and Powell as architects. When construction of the first facility—the pool—began, the terrain consisted of coal refuse.

The initial problem that confronted the architects was the lack of funding provision for enclosed pools in an area where an exposed facility could be effective for only three months of each year. There was a clear requirement for a solution that would provide more than a sometime use and still be affordable and conform to Federal guidelines. An inflatable structure was the answer here, and the limitations of time, cost and gaining approvals required an uncomplicated product which had been tested by standardized manufacture. The available choices could have posed visual and functional problems, but Bohlin and Powell have been innovative in their imaginative adaptation of a commercial object to fit the context of its use.

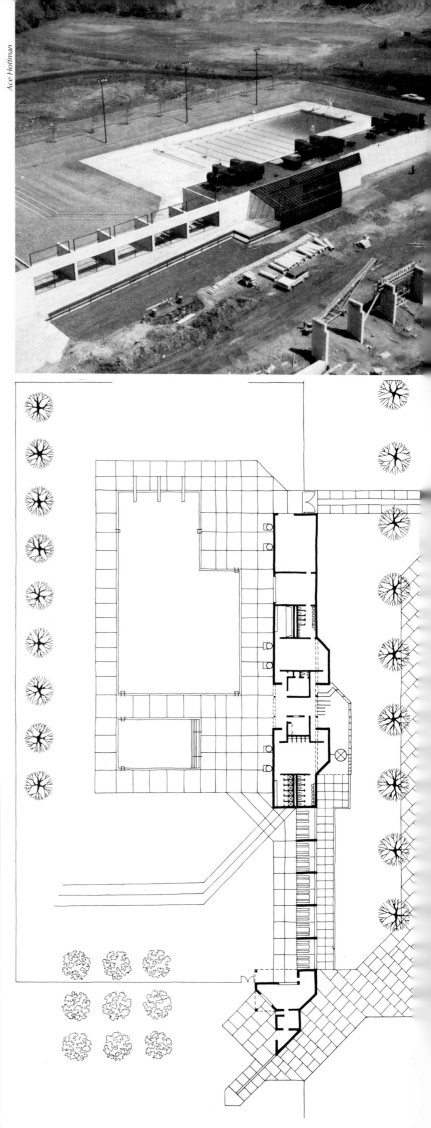

Ace Hoffman

In giving this project a First Honor Award in 1973, the Pennsylvania Society of Architects' jury commented: "Carefully wrought composition in the 'mecho-mod' style. Sensitive land planning and approaches. Designed with a refreshing abandon for simple pleasures." Others, beside Peter Bohlin, were mystified by the exact meaning of "mecho-mod" and whether or not the refreshing abandon might be better applied to the mood of the users rather than to the design process, but the comments do sum up the results fairly accurately.

The linear plan of the permanent structure fulfills two purposes. The first is to direct public traffic in a required progression of access ramp, central lobby, separated dressing rooms and pool, while housing the necessary dressing rooms, offices, pool filtration and air handling equipment, maintenance spaces and air-supported-structure storage. The open spaces beside the ramp contain picnic tables covered with bright yellow canvas awnings, and the "stretching" of the building achieved by the spaces' location have the visual advantage of providing a visually larger and easily identified setting for Coal Street Pool and a hard-edged counterpoint to the rounded shape of the "aquadome" when it is in place. The second reason for the linearity of this concrete frame and exposed-stone-aggregate block building is to relate it to a 800-foot-long walkway which connects the other facilities of playing fields, children's covered play areas (under construction in the photo right) and an ice skating rink planned for the Park. The plan for the Park can be seen overleaf. The playful configuration of the round air-induction pipes (photo, last page, bottom) which provide the air-support for the canvas structure when it is in place, is determined by basic functional requirements. But the architects have not been afraid to take full advantage of the sculptural possibilities by contrasting angular and rounded bands and by painting the sheet metal black on the outside and bright red on the inside. The most economical and tamper-proof location for the air-heaters and blowers was the roof of the permanent building, and the inflatable's manufacturer recommended that the forced air be introduced via the pipes at the bottom of their structure where construction was the strongest and the material least likely to tear. The large size of the ducts was determined by a desire for minimum velocity and thus low draft and noise levels.

Ace Hoffman

There are two "ready-made" structures at the Coal Street Pool. The lobby's glass enclosure (overleaf, bottom) is ordered from a manufacturer's catalog and shares the inflatable's theoretical advantages: testing by previous use, predictable costs and speedy erection. But the architects do not see prefabricated buildings as the answer to all problems, and state that the advantages are not always as real as could be supposed. In the case of the inflatable aquadome, the largest disadvantage may be increased long-term costs which have to be weighed against a first construction cost that is far less than that for a permanent structure. In 1974 the cost of the fabric enclosure was $38,000 to which $24,000 was added for footings, extra heating, airblowers and a storage room bringing the total to $62,000 for the 20,000-square-foot space. The estimated saving over the cost of a permanent enclosure was $218,000. The premium for operating expenses, including added heat, extra help in putting up and taking down the structure and 10-year replacement costs, was estimated to be $11,500 annually or $460,000 over a 40-year-life expectancy for the facility, and it is reasonably certain that these costs will rise. However, an answer to the apparent greater long-term costs here might be found in the interest value of the monies initially saved. For example, $218,000 multiplied by 8 percent and 40 years would total $697,000 leaving a large margin for cost inflation. The above calculations do not take into account the advantages of having the option of an open pool in the summer with only one facility, the appropriately festive atmosphere created by the aquadome or the increased number of possible users when the enclosure is removed. The architects estimate that about 500 people can use the pool at one time in the winter while 2,000 can enjoy the full facilities in the summer. An earth berm has been successful in deflecting the wind during periods of cooler weather when the dome is down. The playful atmosphere is carried into the permanent structure by skylights in the dressing rooms and supergraphics by Mrs. Bohlin.

THE WILKES-BARRE AQUADOME, Wilkes-Barre, Pennsylvania. Owner: *The City of Wilkes-Barre.* Park and recreation planners: *The Allen Organization.* Architects: *Bohlin and Powell—Ronald W. Huntsinger, project architect, Peter Bohlin, partner-in-charge.* Engineers: *Vincent B. Szykman, Inc.* (structural); *Paul H. Yeomans, Inc.* (mechanical/electrical). Landscape architects: *Kennedy and Brown.* Graphics: *Annie Bohlin.* General contractor: *Charles A. Malpass Sons.*

Sandy Nixon

Mark Cohen

Burnside Photography

Sandy Nixon

Sandy Nixon

One of the most interesting visual experiences produced by the aquadome occurs twice a year during the inflation and deflation process (left, top). Forced air is introduced through the visible-round ends of the large pipe-ducts seen without the fabric in place (lower photo, above), and adding a playful atmosphere for the many children using the facility. The open picnic spaces (top) are shielded from the summer sun by bright-yellow awnings and overlook the entrance ramp along which they are located. The pool's permanent ancillary-facilities building is located at the top of the Coal Street Park's masterplan (left) and forms an edge to the Park's central walkway between it and the covered-children's-play arcade bordering athletic fields and playgrounds at the bottom of the plan. The skating rink (overleaf) is located in the lower right hand corner.

Sandy Nixon

THE FULLY DEVELOPED COAL STREET PARK

The previous project, Bohlin and Powell's completed swimming pool under an inflatable structure (far right in plan) was shown with the adjacent municipal recreational facilities under construction. The completed complex is called Coal Street Park. And the other completed structures are shown here.

Along a central walkway (created by the closing of a through street), various playing fields, courts and structures have been arranged at a 45-degree angle to provide true north-south orientation. The largest of the structures (lower left in plan) houses an ice-skating rink in the winter, and is planned to provide a protected area for various other sports in the summer. It consists of both a high roof, supported by enormous rigid steel trusses, and a series of lower spaces at the entrance to house a lobby, offices and changing rooms. The lower structure ties the big "shed" visually to the small-scale play areas

and trellises (left in photo, above) that define the park's walkways. A further tie is achieved by the way in which the shed asymmetrically slopes toward low piers facing the rest of the park.

By contrast, the new children's playground (just above the rink in the plan) is appropriately intimate and small-scaled. A fountain (at top in photo opposite) is placed at the park's entrance— "just as they were used to signify park entrances in the nineteenth century" according to architect Peter Bohlin. But this fountain is active in summer with playing children (photo above). A spillway varies the speed of water.

ICE-A-RAMA, Wilkes-Barre, Pennsylvania. Owner: *The City of Wilkes-Barre.* Architects: *Bohlin and Powell— partner-in-charge: Peter Bohlin; project architect: Ronald Huntsinger.* Associated architects: *The Allen Organization.* Engineers: *Rist-Frost Associates* (structural, mechanical and electrical). General contractor: *Te Sutter Corporation.*

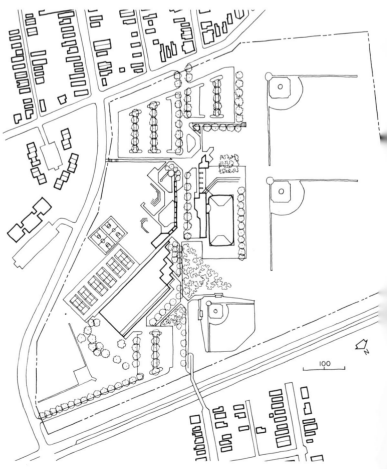

Joseph W. Molitor

Abe Hoffman Studios

A fountain at the park's parking-lot entrance (photo, opposite) is a traditional form here used in new ways—as part of a children's playground (photo, below). From the entrance, visitors are visually led along the central walkway by trellises (to which bright yellow awnings are attached), past a swimming pool to courts for tennis and basketball, playing fields for baseball, soccer and hockey and to the great ice-skating shed (photo, above). The playground is located to the upper left in the site plan.

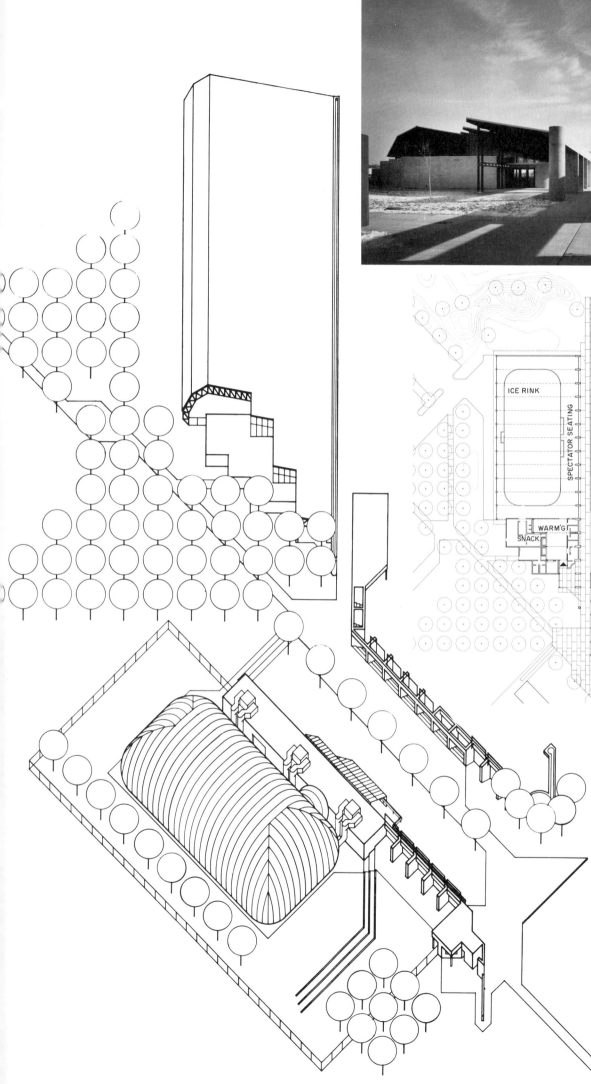

As seen in an isometric view from underneath (opposite page), the large skating shed is tied visually to the smaller-scale trellises that define the park's walkways by presenting a low side to the center of the park. The masonry piers along this side are an extension of the kind of piers used to support the trellises (see photo of entrance above). The large mass of the shed is also screened by the location of the low lobby and administration elements, which are largely roofed by an extension of the shed. The relation of the rink, the central walkway and the older swimming pool (previous project) can be seen in the isometric (left). A red stripe at door-head height leads skaters through the changing room toward the ice (photo, opposite), and augments other graphics.

ICE RINK

SPECTATOR SEATING

TENNIS

WARM'G
SNACK

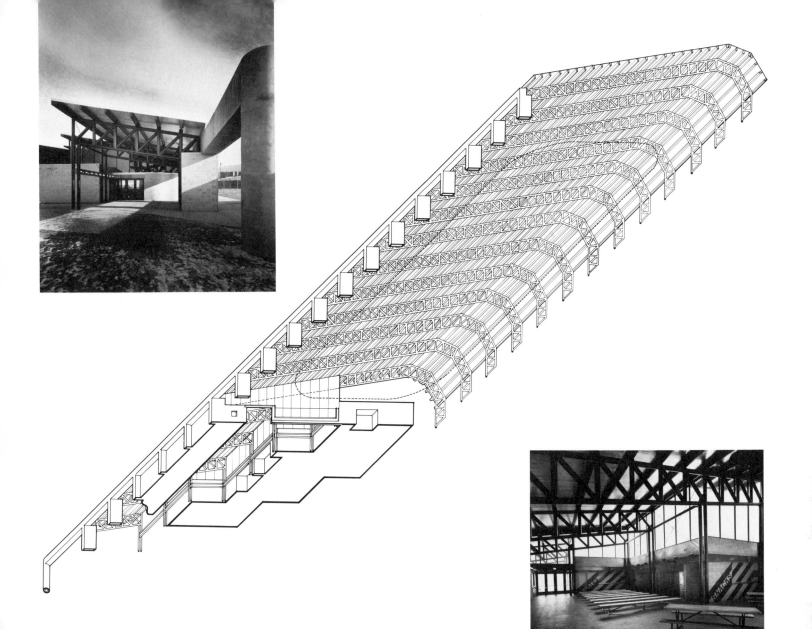

A DIFFERENT KIND OF YOUTH CENTER

The Miami Beach Youth Center is different from many of its predecessors because of the wide variety of activities offered, because those activities are actually what the users wanted, *and* because of the facility's distinctive design. Architects Ferendino/Grafton/Spillis/Candela spent a great amount of time and effort to make sure that the results met the difficult program, and some of the processes are discussed later on. But first, it is interesting to see what their efforts produced.

A surprise here is the diversity of possible activities beside the usual gymnasium and meeting rooms (see plan, overleaf). Within the brightly colored environment, there are constant loud sounds from bowling lanes, pinball machines (located on a mezzanine above the lanes), a juke box and multi-media equipment (located in the smaller round form at the top of the plan, overleaf). Separated from the noisy uses, there are facilities for serious pursuits such as reading, group discussion, musical practice (also located on the mezzanine) and even television programs to augment the local schools' requirements in a more relaxed atmosphere.

The architects point out that—despite the presence of an ice skating rink (to the left of the entrance)—the center conserves energy in ways that hark back to earlier practice than the normally fully enclosed educational facilities in the region. For example, much of the floor area relies on natural ventilation, which of course is only possible all year in such

As viewed from the entrance side (photo, left), the building forms a gateway to a multitude of activities, which include tennis on the roof and swimming in the 75-foot pool. Other activities in the gymnasium are accommodated in spaces that can be open to the outdoors or enclosed, depending on the normally temperate weather (photo above).

subtropical locations. The gymnasium has walls that can be opened up by means of rolling steel doors. And the center's main gathering place is a double-height open "porch" between the swimming pool and gymnasium (photos above and last page).

Almost all of the center's spaces open to each other—either directly or through glass walls. The objects are to encourage interest in all of the activities, to avoid a feeling of isolation when the spaces are under-utilized, and of course to allow surveillance from the control desk. (There are three full-time directors, a supervisor and many part-time directors.)

The 42,300-square-foot facility was built for a cost of $2,300,000 in 1976 on a difficult triangular site, which contained utility ease-

ments that further complicated planning. The building's scale recognizes both the nearby large single-family houses and the fact that the building is institutional in nature. The center's dynamic appearance relies on the molding of traditional construction methods—rather than structural theatrics. It is built in the usual construction manner for the area: poured-in-place concrete frame with stuccoed concrete block infill. The mezzanine and roof (where three tennis courts are located—see aerial photo) are precast concrete double tees.

How did this youth center get to be so different? To a distant viewer, Miami Beach might appear to be the last place in need of government-sponsored social programs and

their facilities, but it has some unique problems. One is a large population of the aging which has retired to a popular mecca of "golden years" sun worship, only to find that their once adequate funds no longer can support them.

Another problem has been the disaffection from the city by the children of often affluent local families. And it was to counter this disaffection that the concept of the youth center was started.

While the very term "youth center" may conjure up images of impoverished neighborhoods and the desire to keep the poor off the streets, the needs here were quite different: to give social cohesion—and hence civic enthusiasm—among contemporaries who might be

otherwise scattered over a broad geographic area. To do this, the center was to provide constructive outlets for pent-up energies, including augmenting school programs and any other activities that might be popular—as well as the traditional athletic facilities.

How is such an unusual facility programmed? To determine what activities were to be housed—as well as an appropriate site—architects Ferendino/Grafton/Spillis/Candela were commissioned to do preliminary research right after approval of the $2.5-million bond issue. A group called "Junior Citizens of Miami Beach" was organized with representation by all local schools, and it acted as an advisory committee to the architects. In the group's

A multitude of recreational equipment is contained in the enclosed parts of the building, and it is made feasible by users paying for damage. Over the bowling lanes (near the entrance) a mezzanine accommodates practice rooms, pinball machines and tables for billiards and paddle tennis (photo, left). A lounge, toward the rear of the building, has tables for study and snacks (photo below).

POOL

LCKS

KIT.

LCKS

LOUNGE

MULTI-PURPOSE AREA

PLAY

SKATING RINK

BOWLING LANES

GYM

N

20

name, a survey was sent to all students between 9 and 18 years of age, and its first question concerned just what was perceived by the potential users when the term "youth center" was mentioned. Aside from the answer: "a place of our own," their perception was close to that of the original intention: to create an atmosphere for social cohesion. The need for the center was emphasized by almost twenty per cent of the respondents stating "nothing" in answer to what they did in their free time.

Other questions involved interests in activities not accommodated by existing local facilities (the consensus included swimming, bowling, tennis, karate, billiards, gymnastics, relaxation, concerts, "rap" sessions and—surprisingly—ice skating) and who should use the facility ("teens," "pre-teens" or both—the consensus was both). Another question concerned the desirable location of the proposed facilities, and the majority answer was a generous "anywhere." The last answer left the architects with a long, detailed search to determine a site. This was finally chosen on the edge of a golf course near two of the larger local schools and public transportation routes.

MIAMI BEACH YOUTH CENTER, Miami Beach, Florida. Owner: *City of Miami Beach.* Architects and engineers: *Ferendino/Grafton/Spillis/Candela—partner-in-charge: Edward Grafton; project manager: Jose Corbato; project architect: Julio Grabiel; interior and graphic designer: Howard Snoweiss and Juan Lezcano.* General contractor: *Seldin Construction Co.*

The "junior citizens" of Miami Beach
have a sparkling new facility that is intended
to bring them together as a cohesive group
—and hence keep them in the community.
To serve its particular function, the building
differs from traditional concepts
in many interesting ways. The image is vibrant;
the possible activities are many and varied.
And most important, the building is
what the users really wanted.

A NATIONAL PARK SERVICE STABLE
BY ARCHITECTS HARTMAN-COX

Noting that most stables have been built without architects, Warren Cox describes the kind of contribution that architects can make—in this case, to a public stable in Washington, D.C.'s Rock Creek Park. Built within a limited budget competitive with the usual pre-engineered structure, this building is a fitting statement for its prominent position in the nation's capital. The basic form is a simple rectangle with a four-way shed roof, which has been altered only enough to accommodate differing internal functions and to provide visual interest and an appropriate sense of scale. For instance, the angled projecting walls allow mechanical equipment to pass through the doors easily, and the lower extensions of the sloping roofs provide desirable ceiling heights in offices and other ancillary spaces.

Cox describes as the origin for the design the great eighteenth-century tithe barns of Europe—even to the section with its clerestory lighting that is similar

to sections found in the older structures. Here, the clerestory took on new importance because of the limitations on lower-level windows caused by the fear of vandalism. The 220-foot-long building has been placed to avoid the extensive cutting of trees and to follow contour lines, thus avoiding undesirable grade changes. Two types of stalls for a total of 40 horses are contained within the 17,000 square feet of area; these are respectively for horses that are leased and those that are boarded.

The wood structure is sheathed in wood board-and-batten siding, painted bright red; the trim is painted white. Altogether, the building is an interesting combination of design vocabulary that echoes both its urban location and its more rural function.

NATIONAL PARK SERVICE STABLE, Washington, D.C. Architects: *Hartman-Cox Architects.* Engineers: *Alfred Kraas Associates* (structural); *Syska & Hennessy* (mechanical). Consultant: *H. Stewart Treviranus* (stable).

A building with a normally-rural function in the center of a city, this stable visually expresses both its function and location with remarkable assurance. A central entrance to control access, also admits tractors that supply hay to the lofts on the second level. Low-level fenestration was limited because of concern over vandalism, and is augmented by the clerestory windows—also important for ventilation. The large round window indicates the entrance, and is a "sign" that indicates the building's function by association with historic imagery.

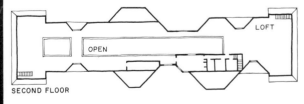

SECOND FLOOR

LOFT

OPEN

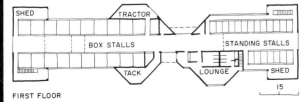

FIRST FLOOR

SHED   TRACTOR
BOX STALLS   STANDING STALLS
TACK   LOUNGE   SHED

15

123

R. CROSBY KEMPER JR. MEMORIAL ARENA

C.F. Murphy Associates, Architects

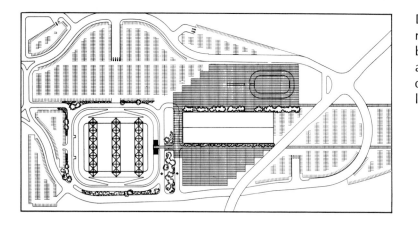

Despite a recent well-publicized mishap with the roof deck of this Kansas City landmark, the building remains remarkable for its almost awesome muscularity of design. Now that the dust has settled, it is well worth an impartial look for its design qualities alone.

Paul Kivett photos

In an otherwise non-luxurious interior, special spectator suites, photo below, and an Arena Club add an uncertain note of elegance. The concourse level, photo left, provides general circulation and entry to the seating area at about mid-level. Graphics convey their information easily and colorfully. Throughout the interiors, the basic palette of colors remains consistent.

The arena's most salient design feature, of course, is the series of three exposed triangular roof trusses that are 27 feet deep and spaced at 153 feet on center. These massive structural elements are tubular sections with diameters that vary from 48 inches for the top chord, to 30 inches for web members, and 36 inches for bottom chords. Wall thicknesses for these sections range between ¼ inch and one inch. The weight of this structural system is 23½ psf and its cost (built before the 1976 increases) was $8.22 per sq ft. After careful testing with models, the beautiful joinery shown in the photo and drawings at right was developed by the architects. The joint, designed to be watertight, is created by the intersection of stiffener plates, the largest having a thickness of 2 inches. The top chord of the truss has a strength of 46 ksi and an actual load, at any midpoint between two joints, of about 28 ksi.

Supporting these sections and transferring their load to grade are concrete pilings driven 60 feet into the earth. These pilings were placed at a slight incline to resist the outward thrust of the trusses. The piling caps, visible in the photo below, are smoothly tapered above grade to provide an elegant base to receive the loads. Within this framework is the arena enclosure itself, a structure clad in metal panels mounted on steel mullions and girts spaced 18 feet and 15 feet on centers respectively. The panels, then costing $3.50 per square foot, were a standard industrial product including both fiber glass insulation and an inner liner. The architects developed a special extrusion to accentuate the panel joints visually and, at the same time, to provide a means for thermal expansion.

A secondary system of bar joists and trusses, visible in the sections, is suspended from the main superstructure and carries a standard metal deck. The section also reveals that the arena sits squarely on an earth berm created from dirt moved during excavation for the building's lowest level. Landscaped along its cleanly beveled edge, the berm provides a pedestrian way around the entire building at concourse level.

Like any contemporary sports facility, Kemper Arena is designed for flexibility. Though neither of its two professional teams—the NBA *Kansas City Kings* and NHL *Kansas City Scouts*—now draws to capacity, the Arena can accommodate up to 16,000 for hockey or 18,000 for basketball. The first few rows of seats are retractable and an insulated wood floor can be put down over the ice floor in three to four hours. Three feet of tanbark is required on the floor during the American Royal Horse and Livestock Show, which is presented here annually. Other uses to which the Arena will be put are track and field meets,

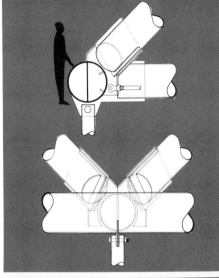

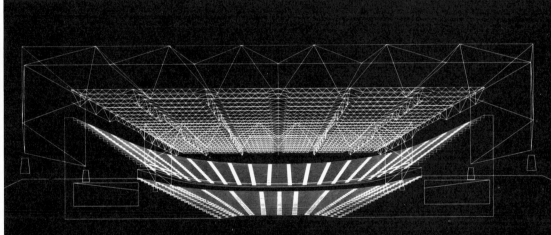

COMPUTER DRAWING

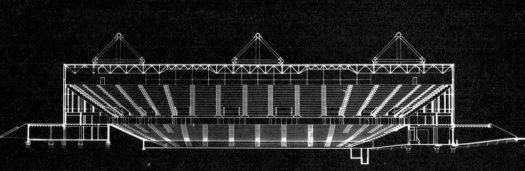

LONGITUDINAL SECTION

TRANSVERSE SECTION

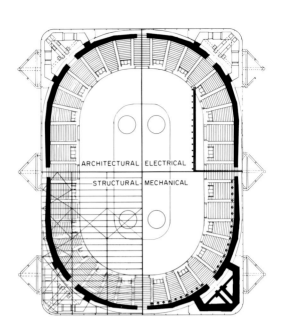

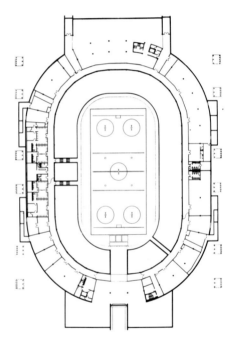

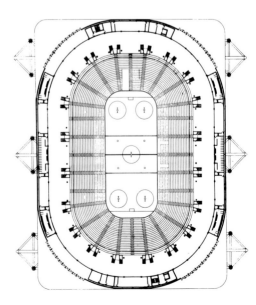

ARCHITECTURAL ELECTRICAL
STRUCTURAL MECHANICAL

music and trade shows as well as conventions of various types. Each of these events, with widely varying functional requirements, will test the Arena's flexibility to the utmost. Sightlines have been carefully worked out so that every spectator has an unobstructed view whether the focus of action be center ice or overhead in the sweeping arcs of aerial acts. The maximum distance from the most remote seat to the center of the Arena is 200 feet in the long axis.

Inside, the building has a lively, hard-working character entirely appropriate to its recreational use. Partitions are mostly ground face block and floors are concrete. Mechanical and structural components are left exposed and painted yellow. The seating is painted a bright blue. A measure of acoustical control is achieved with a fiberboard ceiling suspended from the metal deck.

The architects' first instincts had inclined them toward a stainless steel exterior panel. When initial cost made this idea impractical, an important visual decision had to be made. The problem was whether to express the spidery structure as one element and the enclosure as another by painting each a different color. After careful study of several models, the architects decided to paint both elements white, a decision that softened the mechanistic character of the building considerably and came at no expense to its design clarity. The function of the massive trusses, after all, needed little underscoring.

Construction on the Kemper Arena began in late May of 1973. Owing to the compressed construction schedule, work had to proceed rapidly. The building was largely completed in November 1974 though it remained to add wind baffles at the exterior doors and special railings to control crowd surge. Not only was

construction completed on schedule in spite of a two-month delay caused by strikes, the building came in at its budgeted $10.2 million. Changes, requested by the owners as the multi-use character of the building became more pronounced, added approximately $3.2 million in addition.

The constraints of budget and time notwithstanding, Kemper Arena looks thought-out both in its conception and in its detail. It is no less of interest for its structural elegance than it is as a background for the wide range of sporting entertainments that it was designed to house.

R. CROSBY KEMPER JR. MEMORIAL ARENA, Kansas City, Missouri. Architects and engineers: *C. F. Murphy Associates—Helmut Jahn, partner-in-charge; James Goettsch, project architect.* Landscape architects: *Parks and Recreation, Kansas City.* Consultants: *Coffeen, Gatley and Associates* (acoustical). Contractor: *J. E. Dunn Construction Company.*

STADIUM GRANDSTANDS "FLOAT" ON AIR IN HAWAII

Perhaps the most familiar application of air-film technology is the Hovercraft—lifted above the water by a huge fan and moving swiftly in a cloud of spray. But never has it solved a movement problem quite as massive as conversion of the stands at Aloha Stadium (designed by Charles Luckman Associates): four movable grandstands, a total of 28,000 seats and 7,000 tons, must be moved to differing configurations (photos above) to accommodate football, baseball, soccer, and special events. The principle is simple: a thin film of air serves as a lubricant between the load and the surface to eliminate friction. Beneath each section (see drawing at right), 26 air transporters contain clusters of elongated donut-shaped air bearings. When a central air compressor pumps air to the transporters through underground pipes, the bearings inflate, lifting the load about one inch and then bleeding a .004-in. film of air around the bearing perimeters so the sections can move on the tracks. As each stand "floats," a man operates a hydraulic control console that walks the sections along the curved beams attached to the runways and drives them into place, where they are locked. Each section can be moved by only one man in approximately 25 minutes; and the entire stadium can be totally converted in half a day. The air-film system is built and installed by Rolair Systems.

Williams Photography

. . . AND "WALK" ON WATER IN DENVER

At the Mile High Stadium in Denver, designers Daniel, Mann, Johnson, & Mendenhall—Phillips, Reister added two new grandstands—and a similar conversion problem had to be solved. This load was heavier—23,000 seats and 5,000 tons divided between two sections. And here, a water system designed by Aero-Go, Inc. was chosen. (The company's air bearings were used for San Francisco's BART turntables.) Mounted in steel transporters at 52 support points, the water bearings have flexible and replaceable high-strength fabric diaphragms that swell, and then release a .003-in. fluid film. The water is supplied at 4,000 gallons per minute, and can be recirculated from the runways to the 60,000-gallon storage tank. With a stand "raised," it takes only 1 lb of horizontal force to move 1,000 lbs of vertical load. The hydraulic-jack system completes the entire move in an hour and a half.

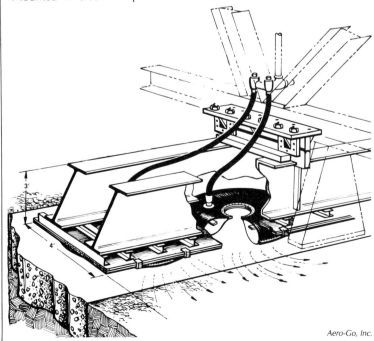

Aero-Go, Inc.

CHAPTER FOUR

BUILDINGS AND FACILITIES FOR CULTURAL PURSUITS: MUSEUMS, VISITORS' CENTERS, A THEATER AND OTHERS

This chapter is notably different from the others. First and most prominently, there is the almost wild diversity of building types, as befits the increasing diversity and—some may say—segmentation of national cultural interests. As discussed in the preface, examples here range from a relatively modest museum and visitor's center adjacent to Gunston Hall in Virginia (designed by architects Philip Ives Associates) to the massive Georges Pompidou National Center of Art and Culture in Paris (designed by architects Piano & Rogers). The one facility for the performing arts shown, The Festival Theater in Caesarea, Israel has an unknown architect and in fact is not a building at all; it is an ancient Roman open air theater adapted by designers George Izenour Associates to the requirements of contemporary concert acoustics.

Another re-use of a somewhat newer structure is architects Holabird & Roots' adaption for the Chicago Cultural Center of the massive and splendid old Chicago Public Library, built in 1897. Another is architects Gunn & Meyerhoff's renovation of the long-unused, modest Savannah railroad station as a center for visitors come to savor the city's historic delights. Architect Edward Larrabee Barnes' work for the New York Botanical Garden is more strictly renovation—while architects Maki and Associates' National Aquarium is a bold new statement in contemporary architecture. Similarly, architects Mitchell/Giurgola Associates' Casa Thomas Jefferson in Brasilia is a contemporary statement that lends some humane qualities to a sometimes bleak environment. Each building (or facility) is unique in its purpose.

Two other differences from other chapters are that several of the buildings are built abroad, and—because several are major architectural statements of the decade or involve important design concepts—that their explanations are rather longer than usual. This is especially true of the piece written by William Marlin in 1978 to assess the results of the use of the Pompidou Center.

Even had this chapter stuck to only those buildings built in the United States, it would have been impossible to cover the broad spectrum of what governments have built to accommodate pursuits. Not only is there such a wide spectrum of these pursuits, but—by the nature of this type of building—the true art of architecture tends to reflect most strongly the particular cultural differences and philosophies of the users.

A VISITORS' CENTER FOR AN HISTORIC HOUSE

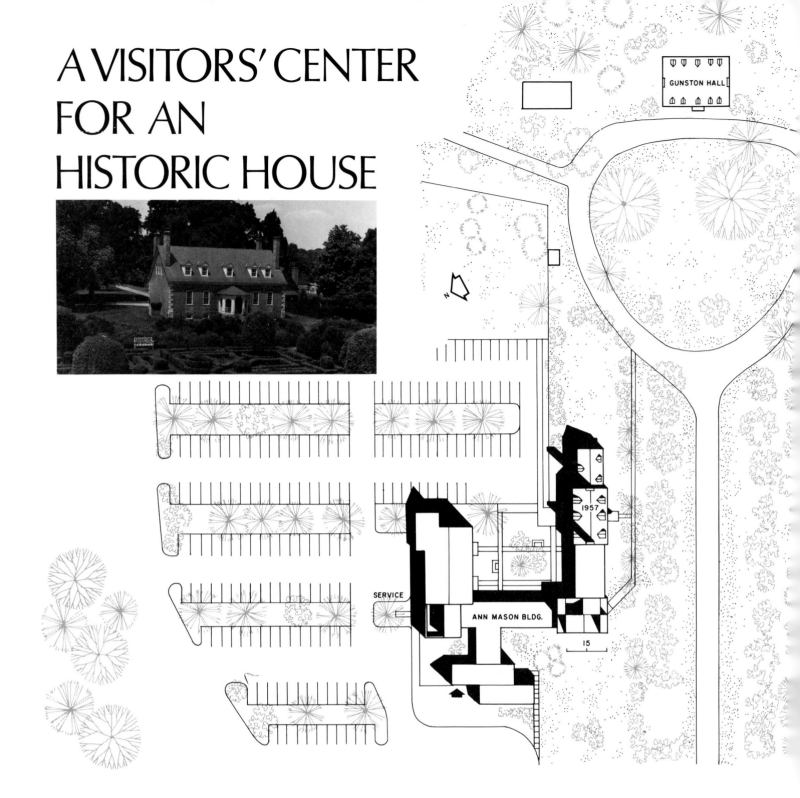

With growing numbers of tourists at traditional and newly established historic sites, such as Gunston Halls' visitors' center shown here, the problem of housing ancillary functions is becoming well worth examining. Often the contemporary buildings that will house rest rooms, archives, offices, tour-marshaling spaces and exhibition galleries are much larger than any historic building that may be the focus of the site. As the new building must be within a short walk, it can threaten to visually overpower and hence destroy the very object of the tour.

Previous approaches to the problem have not always been successful, as in the case of several small Presidential birthplaces that have been almost completely enshrined in mausoleum-type enclosures in this century. More recently, such new construction has taken two basic directions. New buildings can be hidden in the woods, behind berms or even underground. Or perhaps more controversial, such new buildings can be highly visible, but are designed to be compatible. The approach is more controversial because it can be argued that *any* visible new construction will appreciably alter the context in which the historic structure was previously seen.

Nonetheless, architect Philip Ives has used the latter approach at historic Gunston Hall in Virginia (site plan, above), and has produced a very interesting result. Largely, his decision was dictated by existing conditions, which provided the opportunity to make the Hall's Ann Mason visitors' center a highly visible, but sympathetic building.

Perhaps controversial, new buildings at historic sites can be highly visible and still compatible

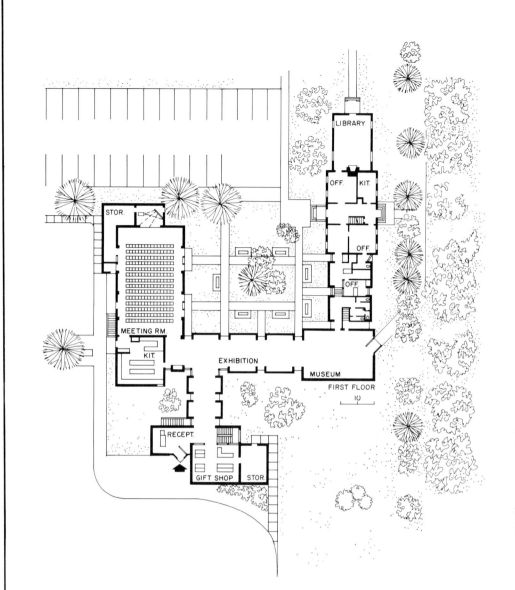

The visitors' center in Lorton, Virginia for the small eighteenth-century home of Revolutionary War figure George Mason is really a large addition to a recent archive-office building. The latter modest structure was conceived as an out building of the main house in 1957 in a similar style. It occupies a highly visible site on the approach road close to the main historic structure, Gunston Hall, (see site plan, opposite).

As the "out building" was the result of a private contribution, it could not be easily scrapped. And the logistics of greatly expanded public services required that the functions of both buildings be combined. Accordingly, architect Philip Ives has produced one large "out building" that is five times the size of the original. The new portion contains a large auditorium, exhibition and reception spaces and rest rooms in a fairly large building that looks like a series of small ones. At first glance from the entrance drive it actually appears as a group of small scaled farm structures that might have been there all along. Except, the new buildings are clearly from the present era.

The roof slopes echo rural Georgian lines. And the roofing material is slate, the walls are brick—both materials being the same as those of the eighteenth-century Gunston Hall. Careful attention has been given to keeping the immediately visible volumes of the new buildings from competing with the 1950s structure, which—no relic in itself—has gained compatibility through aging. The fenestration in the new construction also avoids competition by being either similar in proportion to the old, or so completely different so as to defy comparison (such as the clerestories). The construction is masonry bearing wall with either wood or steel roof framing, depending on length of spans. The 1977 construction cost was about $925,000. Clearly the building is highly visible. But it is so sympathetically designed that it is a positive complement to the landmark which it serves.

ANN MASON BUILDING, Lorton, Virginia. Owner: *The Commonwealth of Virginia*. Architects: *Philip Ives Associates*—architect-in-charge: *Frank Bachrack*. Engineers: *Throop D. Feiden* (structural); *Harry Bond* (mechanical/electrical). Consultants: *Wheel-Gavan* (lighting); *Thomas Condit* (landscape architect); *George Kaplan* (cost). General contractor: *Whyte Construction Company*.

Taylor Lewis, photos

The interiors of the visitors' center utilize the highly pitched roofs in two ways that are more typical of the mid-twentieth century than of their eighteenth century derivation. The first way is to simply leave the newly created internal space exposed, as is done in the lobby (photo, bottom left). The second is to provide a "checkerboard" pattern of lower horizontal ceiling contrasted with ceilings that slope to clerestories. The museum space (photo above) is the last part of a tour marshaling area, from which groups leave to see Gunston Hall by the door shown at the left. The door (as well as that at the main entrance) is angled to provide a subtle nudge toward the intended direction of the tours.

The Georges Pompidou National Center of Art and Culture has been open two years.
It has perplexed, possessed, repulsed, inspired, traumatized, entertained, and
won. This amalgam of activity and emotion isn't out of character. No, it's . . .

A Building of Paris

This city of light has glowed with many grand horizontals. Now there are those of the Georges Pompidou National Center of Art and Culture, which was thought up by the late French President in 1969, and which is commonly called Beaubourg, after its old neighborhood, a juicy jumble of 17th-, 18th-, and 19th-century buildings with the consistency of onion soup.

Beaubourg's grand horizontals are, by comparison, pyrotechnic, housing a colorful melange of activities, emotions, images, and information. They are gotten up like bridges, six of them stacked together, making lofty layers of space, a million square feet of it. All this stacks up to a height of 138 feet, taking up about half of a ten-acre site which, from the 1930s, was a parking lot—the other half now being a public square with a great many things going on in it. The result is that Beaubourg, held up with a system of exposed structural details, strung and hung with a system of exposed mechanical entrails, rambunctiously pokes its piping-cool bulk, 550 feet long, 197 feet wide, just above the Right Bank's roof tops, from which, a year after completion, many Parisians, as rambunctious, are still trying to shout the building down.

Which figures. Parisians have never drawn too severe a distinction between loving and loathing things (or each other), and the capital has practically made a career of carping about Beaubourg's pre-emptory scale, its fever-pitch fabric of columns, trusses, fancy joints, and criss-crossed bracing, its polychromatic plumbing. Absolutely nothing, along with absolutely everything, has been left to the imagination. Which is as Parisian as a building can get.

And so, having said, these past few years, that they were not about to stand still for such a funny-looking piece of architecture, people aren't. Parisians aren't. People from other parts of France, and Europe, aren't. People from all over the world aren't. What they are doing, by way of not standing still for Beaubourg, is showing up, by the thousands, every day of the week, from ten in the morning to ten at night. It is not just that there is a lot to see and do in, certainly around, the place. It is that people, even those as charmingly contentious as Parisians, have been forced (or inspired) to admit, if only deep down, that this funny-looking piece of architecture *is* in scale.

Mon Dieu. In scale with what? With the long-built-up character of its physical context? The close-grained medieval district of Le Marais

edges Beaubourg's site, hard against the building to the east, right across the Rue du Renard. The Boulevard de Sebastopol edges its site, over a hop, skip, and jump across the new public square, to the west, with the former site of Les Halles, the old central marketplace, a couple blocks beyond that. As to this context, which must be said to include the River Seine, Notre Dame, and the Louvre, a few blocks southward, Beaubourg, having been scorned as a colossal incongruity, is a lot more congenial and consolidating a presence, however pyrotechnic those grand horizontals may look, than its harshest critics feared (or hoped).

But Beaubourg is in scale in another sense, in scale with as crucial and telling a context— that is, with long-built-up characteristics of popular sentiments, attitudes, and urges. It has been said that Beaubourg is a meeting between the tastes and preoccupations of a president— between these and the aspirations, "still latent," of the French people. Aspirations may not be the right word. Inclinations is a more accurate one.

It is likely that Pompidou understood this better than anyone. A center of art and culture, were it really to awaken those "still latent" aspirations, would have to appeal to something in the French people that was *already* awake— not to the conventional idea of art and culture, not to the conventional image of what a museum looks like or feels like. It would have to be, visually and functionally and socially, a jugular, throbbing—something to go for. Beaubourg is that, a pleasingly perverse, but wholly honest, expression of the old French passion, as architect Philip Johnson recently quipped, of "going all the way."

In a city where dalliance is a devotion, Beaubourg, rumbling in the urban belly, is a source of entertainment, as much as of enlightenment; of relaxation, as much as of revelation. All the stuff of art and culture is sitting, hanging, or leaning around in those vast spaces inside, or in that vast space outside. None of it is stuffed down anyone's throat. People, acting as much on impulse as anything resembling artistic and cultural aspirations, can stare, study, saunter, bumping into, reeling back from, or embracing the evidence of avant-garde adventure.

But to most—and Pompidou, the avant-garde art buff, understood this too—this public experience works because Beaubourg, quite deliberately, works more like a shopping emporium, an amusement park, or a street festival. The president, in a proposition as much

political as cultural, wanted to bring the French along, expecting that a populist draw, full of fun and games, would subtly swing them toward a warmer, more responsive feeling for serious cultural expression. So he put one of the world's most amazing, efficient bureaucracies to work in coming up with a place which people, either hopping mad or helplessly mesmerized by its looks, could not ignore.

It is wide of the mark to assert, as it has been, that Beaubourg is a piece of Gaullist condescension, that its administrators and staff are force-feeding art to the public, that its fun-and-games atmosphere really talks down to the so-called average man, or that the establishment was, and is, bound and determined to teach him a thing or two about what is serious cultural expression and what isn't.

Beaubourg, as a sign of France's, particularly Paris's, hoped for re-emergence as the world's fundamental font of inquiry, experiment, and innovation, could only be believable, in this egalitarian time, if public participation and experience were the integral, integrating force. In this, it was that so-called average man who had taught the establishment, both the political one and the cultural one, a thing or two.

So a fire was set—again, despite the rhetoric of officialdom, not under public aspirations, but under public inclinations, including the inclination to be argumentative, to feign horror, to heckle, to be hostile to strangers, intrigued by them, and the inclination to have a ball. If there is any irony in this fire that was set by Beaubourg, it is that all of the criticism of its architecture was actually a sign of growing fascination for what was afoot.

There was a facetiousness on both sides of the construction fence, with very few people sitting on the fence itself. And in France, even facetiousness must be affected in a grandiose way. What France has gotten is, more than a place where the spirit can soar, a baring of its social and political soul. Beaubourg is a deft misalliance of both avant-garde and reactionary motives, brought off with managerial precision, psychological savvy, and showmanship. The most spontaneous and the most discerning tastes have been seen to. The height of contemporary creation has all the head room it will ever need, as do those throngs of people who would just as soon not let on that they have aspirations, "still latent," for scaling those heights.

Not surprisingly, the world design contest of 1971, which Pompidou called an "international competition of ideas," was staged with great aplomb. The embassies and consulates of France, practically everywhere, threw lavish parties to kick the contest off. Architects rented Citroens to drive up in, or at least some did. Subsequently, 681 schemes were received from 71 countries, which were gone over by an international jury, including Philip Johnson, Oscar Niemeyer, Jean Prouve, who was the chairman, plus a number of big-name museum officials from around Europe. The winning scheme, as anyone at all involved or even interested in architecture knows by now, was by Renzo Piano, of Italy, and Richard Rogers, of England—teamed, in turn, with the London engineering firm of Ove Arup & Partners.

Rogers has said that he was initially hesitant about entering the competition because he didn't want to have any part in building just another elitist enclave. By way of dramatizing their belief that a center of art and culture shouldn't be that, and maybe in the hope that the jury would get their message, these architects, almost alone out of all the entries, deliberately designed a public experience, a cage for the age of multi-media and mass-circulation. Times Square, they compared it to, with some of the British Museum tossed in. Almost alone, too, out of all the entries, the four major components—a museum of modern art, a public information library, an industrial design center, an institute for musical and acoustical research—were all brought together in their scheme, like the interlocking circuits of a four-track cassette. Instant play-back, constant feedback, with the four components routinely plugging into each other, and the public plugging into them all. This French Dream Machine was a dare, which the jury not only took, but also delighted in. Pompidou, predicting a storm of controversy, scarcely concealed his own (the plot was thickening).

Beaubourg's architecture is deeply embedded in the theoretical aspic of the 1960s, that jelled in the English molds of Archigram, mainly, along with the metabolic noodle-making experiments of various Italians and Japanese. Archigram's high priests, occupied with process, change, and the expendability of all things, were insistent that a building or even a whole city, is the same as a TV dinner. Flexibility and functionality were measured by the ease with which something could be gotten, consumed or used, and then dispensed with. Archigram's cities, remember, *walked.* Its structures whirred, snorted, batting their *brise soleil* in

assorted cybernetic rites. It was an extremely serious movement. It really was. And it took the opportunity of Beaubourg to awaken these assumptions from the megastructural stupor into which the Archigram set had seemingly lulled itself.

This building is both the illumination and the immolation of those assumptions. Piano + Rogers has been harder on itself than any of the building's detractors in fighting to make those assumptions work, testing and adapting and changing and perfecting. Half of their team's energies was spent fighting to keep the basic kinetic character of the concept intact; the rest, to make that concept answerable to the hard facts of the situation. As much as some people have said that they fear the possibility, Beaubourg will not be casting a mold for the future, at least a formal mold. Little Beaubourgs will not be seen rising around the world. It's too skillful a eulogy.

Their "live center of information *is* living, and will continue to. But its true significance is misjudged if it is studied only as the vindication of a theoretical position. It is possible to mislay oneself, as the poet Rimbaud, saying so, knew full well. And that goes for movements as well as men. Piano + Rogers, answering to the spirit as well as specifics of the Beaubourg challenge, has not mislaid its values. Certain perceptions of a movement they learned from were put to work. But beyond the vindication of theory, Beaubourg's unique program brought about an enlargement of experience—their experience, not to mention the cultural experience of the public that they were *consciously* creating for.

Perhaps one of the most crucial aspects of this maturity is that they were put in mind, as the rest of us might well be, that theory is not something, limited to formal and technical propositions, that sits smugly outside the world of actual experience. Theory is rooted in it.

It so happens that the public experience of art and culture, or perhaps it would be better to say the art and culture of public experience, motivated the architects as much as any set of tenets within the traditions of so-called modern architecture. That Beaubourg represents a conjunction, and a rare conjunction at that, between such perceptions and a particular theoretical starting point is a measure of the architects' accomplishment because, finally, it is the architecture's incorporation of the public, and the public's very perception of itself as Beaubourg is experienced, which permeates the design, in all of its dimensions.

If Marcel Proust was at all accurate in saying that the only paradise is paradise lost, it may be as accurate, especially in the case of Beaubourg, to say the same of paradigms. What "models" of perception and application are being sought when one reads a newspaper, listens to a radio, watches television? There is a little of all of these in, and around, Beaubourg. The media that people have used to find out things, these are the dimensions that the architecture measures. Or the dimensions that the architecture allows people to measure, uncoercively letting them in on many different levels of information and insight.

An example is the Museum of Modern Art at Beaubourg, which is headed by Pontus Hulten, of Sweden, who used to head the Moderna Muséet in Stockholm. The need for such a museum has been talked about for many years, and at one point, the late Andre Malraux, whose death came poignantly one month before Beaubourg's opening, wanted to build one by Le Corbusier—but on the outskirts of Paris. Le Corbusier, wanting to reinforce the center of the city, in obvious contrast to what he wanted to do to it in the 1920s, cooled on Malraux's patrician and escapist concept of what a museum should be.

Hulten, who has allowed that the throngs visiting Beaubourg sometimes drive him to distraction, believes, however, that if the hallowed cult-like calm of the traditional museum has been lost, so much the better. "The partitioning of art, literature, science, and music is a notion which life itself has gone far beyond," Hulten insists. "A true science of information is now beginning to develop in correlation with the new orientation of science and the social sciences; art history, communications, cybernetics, linguistics, and semiology have restated the concepts of theory, history, space, and time—along with concepts of the symbol—all in new terms. We are moving toward a society where art will play a great role, which is why this museum is opened to disciplines that were once excluded by museums, and which is why it is open to the largest possible public." That public, throughout Beaubourg, is already wearing the carpet thin.

Round about Hulten's museum, now the largest one for modern art in Europe, there is not only a stunning permanent collection, dating from the turn of the century, but wide-open ranges of one-man and thematic exhibitions, along with sections for both permanent and temporary exhibitions of graphic art, photography, films, and video-tape experimentation. Conference rooms, information booths, rest areas, projection rooms, research and archival facilities are arranged around the vast floor area. Any of these elements, along with the various shows, can be rearranged at any time. Even the tidy little men's and women's rooms can be.

If there are times when this museum of modern art seems (and sounds) like a giant fact-finding, image-flashing research center which just happens to have a lot of rotating art exhibitions hanging around, Beaubourg also has a *real* research center, its public information library, which is headed by Jean Pierre Seguin. In contrast to France's many libraries, almost all of which have been off-limits to the public, this one is an off-the-street, on-the-spot resource for anyone doing anything from a book report on Cézanne to a state study on the psychological effects of wall paper decorations on the efficiency of bureaucrats. Books, periodicals, slides, records, microfilm and microfiche, films and video cassettes in this "university of the people," and it really *is* working as such, are supplemented by a current events hall, located on Beaubourg's ground levels, where one can leaf through or buy just about any newspaper or magazine now being published.

Seguin is a lot more frank, and congenial, than most of Beaubourg's chiefs in acknowledging the relationship of his operation to American precedent. "The liberty and movement in the libraries of the U.S. have always been an inspiration to me," Seguin says. "In fact, those libraries are among the best examples of the success of American civilization. We went over to study the best things that have been done, came back, copied them—and just perhaps, are doing it even better."

Many of the more pedagogical types in library science have criticized this approach, comparing it to a discount house or fast-food-for-thought operation. But Seguin believes that the informational, invitational atmosphere, though hardly "home-like" as he also asserts, will bear up under the 4000-person-per-day ordeal and, as importantly, prove that popular accessibility to knowledge does not have to mean the debasement of serious scholarship. The most casual self-improver, absorbed student, or plodding professor can get off by themselves, what with quiet reading rooms, with various hierarchies of solitude, scattered through out the open stacks. Seguin acknowl-

edges that careful programming of his library's many diverse, often overlapping functions was necessary to avoid what he calls "conflict" with the architecture—meaning, and this is something that is being reckoned with throughout Beaubourg, that floors this big, enshrining the notion of flexibility, can be a problem when having to arrange for activities, as in a library, which really should be off by themselves.

Beaubourg's Center for Industrial Design, a third major element of the operation, is one of the most out-going—dealing with cities and towns throughout France, in both an educational and advisory way, on matters of public design, from transportation systems and graphics to community development plans. Research facilities and exhibition programs are giving the public unprecedented access to practical, immediately useful information about product design on every level of experience— almost a *Consumers Guide* approach. And both the philosophical and applied aspects of architectural and urban design have, for the first time, been given a laboratory in which to test ideas.

When it comes to testing, the fourth element of Beaubourg, the Institute for the Research and Coordination of Acoustics and Music, is perhaps the most Jules Verne aspect of the place, and, like Nemo's *Nautilus*, it is mostly submerged—in this case, beneath a plaza next to the Church of St. Merri, just south of the main building. Pompidou personally picked up the phone to inspire the return to France of the institute's director, Pierre Boulez, long familiar to American audiences—and one of the authentic innovators in the tradition of Stravinsky, Schoenberg, and Webern. IRCAM, as his institute is called, is not meant to be a classy little cliché of impresarios fooling around with computers, but in the spirit of Boulez, to bring together the tools and perceptions of science with advancing musical theory. Because Boulez doesn't like the conventional concert hall, any more than Pontus Hulten likes the conventional museum, the main feature of IRCAM is a 400-set squared-off *espace de projection*, where the technical, physical, and psychological dimensions of sound are being dealt with.

This structural box, its walls and ceiling composed of adjustable acoustical panels in a pleated configuration, is a musical instrument in itself, and can assume almost any configuration, of either acoustics, instrumentation, or seating. There is no "orchestra" as such, but a

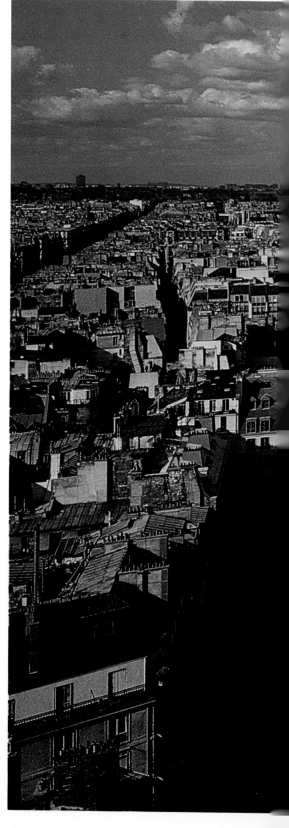

tional competition of ideas," was staged with great aplomb. The embassies and consulates of France, practically everywhere, threw lavish parties to kick the contest off. Architects rented Citroens to drive up in, or at least some did. Subsequently, 681 schemes were received from 71 countries, which were gone over by an international jury, including Philip Johnson, Oscar Niemeyer, Jean Prouve, who was the chairman, plus a number of big-name museum officials from around Europe. The winning scheme, as anyone at all involved or even interested in architecture knows by now, was by Renzo Piano, of Italy, and Richard Rogers, of England—teamed, in turn, with the London engineering firm of Ove Arup & Partners.

Rogers has said that he was initially hesitant about entering the competition because he didn't want to have any part in building just another elitist enclave. By way of dramatizing their belief that a center of art and culture shouldn't be that, and maybe in the hope that the jury would get their message, these architects, almost alone out of all the entries, deliberately designed a public experience, a cage for the age of multi-media and mass-circulation. Times Square, they compared it to, with some of the British Museum tossed in. Almost alone, too, out of all the entries, the four major components—a museum of modern art, a public information library, an industrial design center, an institute for musical and acoustical research—were all brought together in their scheme, like the interlocking circuits of a four-track cassette. Instant play-back, constant feedback, with the four components routinely plugging into each other, and the public plugging into them all. This French Dream Machine was a dare, which the jury not only took, but also delighted in. Pompidou, predicting a storm of controversy, scarcely concealed his own (the plot was thickening).

Beaubourg's architecture is deeply embedded in the theoretical aspic of the 1960s, that jelled in the English molds of Archigram, mainly, along with the metabolic noodle-making experiments of various Italians and Japanese. Archigram's high priests, occupied with process, change, and the expendability of all things, were insistent that a building or even a whole city, is the same as a TV dinner. Flexibility and functionality were measured by the ease with which something could be gotten, consumed or used, and then dispensed with. Archigram's cities, remember, *walked*. Its structures whirred, snorted, batting their *brise soleil* in

assorted cybernetic rites. It was an extremely serious movement. It really was. And it took the opportunity of Beaubourg to awaken these assumptions from the megastructural stupor into which the Archigram set had seemingly lulled itself.

This building is both the illumination and the immolation of those assumptions. Piano + Rogers has been harder on itself than any of the building's detractors in fighting to make those assumptions work, testing and adapting and changing and perfecting. Half of their team's energies was spent fighting to keep the basic kinetic character of the concept intact; the rest, to make that concept answerable to the hard facts of the situation. As much as some people have said that they fear the possibility, Beaubourg will not be casting a mold for the future, at least a formal mold. Little Beaubourgs will not be seen rising around the world. It's too skillful a eulogy.

Their "live center of information *is* living, and will continue to. But its true significance is misjudged if it is studied only as the vindication of a theoretical position. It is possible to mislay oneself, as the poet Rimbaud, saying so, knew full well. And that goes for movements as well as men. Piano + Rogers, answering to the spirit as well as specifics of the Beaubourg challenge, has not mislaid its values. Certain perceptions of a movement they learned from were put to work. But beyond the vindication of theory, Beaubourg's unique program brought about an enlargement of experience—their experience, not to mention the cultural experience of the public that they were *consciously* creating for.

Perhaps one of the most crucial aspects of this maturity is that they were put in mind, as the rest of us might well be, that theory is not something, limited to formal and technical propositions, that sits smugly outside the world of actual experience. Theory is rooted in it.

It so happens that the public experience of art and culture, or perhaps it would be better to say the art and culture of public experience, motivated the architects as much as any set of tenets within the traditions of so-called modern architecture. That Beaubourg represents a conjunction, and a rare conjunction at that, between such perceptions and a particular theoretical starting point is a measure of the architects' accomplishment because, finally, it is the architecture's incorporation of the public, and the public's very perception of itself as Beaubourg is experienced, which permeates the design, in all of its dimensions.

If Marcel Proust was at all accurate in saying that the only paradise is paradise lost, it may be as accurate, especially in the case of Beaubourg, to say the same of paradigms. What "models" of perception and application are being sought when one reads a newspaper, listens to a radio, watches television? There is a little of all of these in, and around, Beaubourg. The media that people have used to find out things, these are the dimensions that the architecture measures. Or the dimensions that the architecture allows people to measure, uncoercively letting them in on many different levels of information and insight.

An example is the Museum of Modern Art at Beaubourg, which is headed by Pontus Hulten, of Sweden, who used to head the Moderna Muséet in Stockholm. The need for such a museum has been talked about for many years, and at one point, the late Andre Malraux, whose death came poignantly one month before Beaubourg's opening, wanted to build one by Le Corbusier—but on the outskirts of Paris. Le Corbusier, wanting to reinforce the center of the city, in obvious contrast to what he wanted to do to it in the 1920s, cooled on Malraux's patrician and escapist concept of what a museum should be.

Hulten, who has allowed that the throngs visiting Beaubourg sometimes drive him to distraction, believes, however, that if the hallowed cult-like calm of the traditional museum has been lost, so much the better. "The partitioning of art, literature, science, and music is a notion which life itself has gone far beyond," Hulten insists. "A true science of information is now beginning to develop in correlation with the new orientation of science and the social sciences; art history, communications, cybernetics, linguistics, and semiology have restated the concepts of theory, history, space, and time—along with concepts of the symbol—all in new terms. We are moving toward a society where art will play a great role, which is why this museum is opened to disciplines that were once excluded by museums, and which is why it is open to the largest possible public." That public, throughout Beaubourg, is already wearing the carpet thin.

Round about Hulten's museum, now the largest one for modern art in Europe, there is not only a stunning permanent collection, dating from the turn of the century, but wide-open ranges of one-man and thematic exhibitions, along with sections for both permanent and temporary exhibitions of graphic art, photography, films, and video-tape experimentation. Conference rooms, information booths, rest areas, projection rooms, research and archival facilities are arranged around the vast floor area. Any of these elements, along with the various shows, can be rearranged at any time. Even the tidy little men's and women's rooms can be.

If there are times when this museum of modern art seems (and sounds) like a giant fact-finding, image-flashing research center which just happens to have a lot of rotating art exhibitions hanging around, Beaubourg also has a *real* research center, its public information library, which is headed by Jean Pierre Seguin. In contrast to France's many libraries, almost all of which have been off-limits to the public, this one is an off-the-street, on-the-spot resource for anyone doing anything from a book report on Cézanne to a state study on the psychological effects of wall paper decorations on the efficiency of bureaucrats. Books, periodicals, slides, records, microfilm and microfiche, films and video cassettes in this "university of the people," and it really *is* working as such, are supplemented by a current events hall, located on Beaubourg's ground levels, where one can leaf through or buy just about any newspaper or magazine now being published.

Seguin is a lot more frank, and congenial, than most of Beaubourg's chiefs in acknowledging the relationship of his operation to American precedent. "The liberty and movement in the libraries of the U.S. have always been an inspiration to me," Seguin says. "In fact, those libraries are among the best examples of the success of American civilization. We went over to study the best things that have been done, came back, copied them—and just perhaps, are doing it even better."

Many of the more pedagogical types in library science have criticized this approach, comparing it to a discount house or fast-food-for-thought operation. But Seguin believes that the informational, invitational atmosphere, though hardly "home-like" as he also asserts, will bear up under the 4000-person-per-day ordeal and, as importantly, prove that popular accessibility to knowledge does not have to mean the debasement of serious scholarship. The most casual self-improver, absorbed student, or plodding professor can get off by themselves, what with quiet reading rooms, with various hierarchies of solitude, scattered through out the open stacks. Seguin acknowl-

edges that careful programming of his library's many diverse, often overlapping functions was necessary to avoid what he calls "conflict" with the architecture—meaning, and this is something that is being reckoned with throughout Beaubourg, that floors this big, enshrining the notion of flexibility, can be a problem when having to arrange for activities, as in a library, which really should be off by themselves.

Beaubourg's Center for Industrial Design, a third major element of the operation, is one of the most out-going—dealing with cities and towns throughout France, in both an educational and advisory way, on matters of public design, from transportation systems and graphics to community development plans. Research facilities and exhibition programs are giving the public unprecedented access to practical, immediately useful information about product design on every level of experience—almost a *Consumers Guide* approach. And both the philosophical and applied aspects of architectural and urban design have, for the first time, been given a laboratory in which to test ideas.

When it comes to testing, the fourth element of Beaubourg, the Institute for the Research and Coordination of Acoustics and Music, is perhaps the most Jules Verne aspect of the place, and, like Nemo's *Nautilus*, it is mostly submerged—in this case, beneath a plaza next to the Church of St. Merri, just south of the main building. Pompidou personally picked up the phone to inspire the return to France of the institute's director, Pierre Boulez, long familiar to American audiences—and one of the authentic innovators in the tradition of Stravinsky, Schoenberg, and Webern. IRCAM, as his institute is called, is not meant to be a classy little cliché of impresarios fooling around with computers, but in the spirit of Boulez, to bring together the tools and perceptions of science with advancing musical theory. Because Boulez doesn't like the conventional concert hall, any more than Pontus Hulten likes the conventional museum, the main feature of IRCAM is a 400-set squared-off *espace de projection*, where the technical, physical, and psychological dimensions of sound are being dealt with.

This structural box, its walls and ceiling composed of adjustable acoustical panels in a pleated configuration, is a musical instrument in itself, and can assume almost any configuration, of either acoustics, instrumentation, or seating. There is no "orchestra" as such, but a

The six lofty levels of the Georges Pompidou National Center of Art and Culture edge enticingly above the Right Bank's roof tops (below). The east side, looking north, hard against the busy Rue du Renard, has a 20-foot-wide zone of exposed structural and mechanical elements (overleaf, top). The close-grained medieval district of Le Marais is immediately east of this (overleaf, below left), and its texture is ironically enhanced by Beaubourg's piping, ducts, and assorted circulatory tubes—red for the movement of people, green for water, blue for air conditioning, and yellow for electricity. The west side, over-looking the new public square (overleaf, below right), is strung with steel-framed, molded-glass tubes that function as corridors and, in the diagonal, as an eye-popping run for escalators. The exposed structure, despite its seemingly frenetic fabric, is a model of simplicity, consistency, and a crafts-manship so thorough as to recall the pioneering feats of French engineers in the 19th Century. Steel in cast components is the basic grammar. Ten-ton, 26-foot-long pin-like cantilevers called *gerberettes* fit around the columns supporting the long lattice beams.

constantly changing group of musicians, scientists (in some cases, one in the same), who are testing new combinations of instruments, sounds, tonalities, and atonalities—the computer being a central investigative tool.

In a way, IRCAM, as relatively isolated as its program is (sound-proofing being a major factor), is also a useful metaphor for Beaubourg as a whole. As innovative as its personnel and instrumentation may be, this "new" music that is being heard, the very nature of sound itself, harkens back to the sensory, symbolic, and social nuances of basic communication—the aural archetypes of ancient, pre-literate man. Beaubourg is an investigative tool, too, in the sense that it is amplifying man's ability to communicate while tapping into the spiritual bedrock that undergirds all creative effort. Post-literate man, as predicted by such apostles of the electronic age as Marshall McLuhan, will find little solace in this atmosphere, as wired as Beaubourg may be for visual excitement. "Artificial intelligence is not yet very intelligent," mused an IRCAM staff member. "Finally, it is *human* comprehension that Beaubourg, with all of its departments and all of its equipment, is meant to expand."

"What do you think of that *thing* in Paris?" has to be the most common question being asked, at least among architects, these days. A great many things that architects, or observers of architecture, have been taught to think, or have come to think, have made it difficult to even consider the possibility of liking "that thing." But like it, despite many previously formed feelings, a lot of people do. What is there about Beaubourg that impels people who *do* spend a lot of time thinking about art and culture to suspend their disdain for it, even as, with most architects especially, they cannot bring themselves to suspend their disdain for the Archigramesque propositions that it is supposed to embody? Put another way, at what point does one's disagreement with a theory give way to a respect for something that, while incorporating theory in formal and technical terms, has obviously transcended those limitations to deal with a larger truth?

Beaubourg's architecture brings us feet to the fire, when it comes to that. First, as strange and far-out as the building seems when coming upon it, Beaubourg is not this century's reach for the next. It may well be, in fact, this century's reach for the last. And this, too, involves more than just architectural pre-

cedents, such as the wide-span halls of the great 19th-century expositions. In other words, Beaubourg is more than an amplification of the material and methodological wherewithal of an earlier day. even as its own wide spans clearly *élan*. No, what makes Beaubourg a powerful presence in architectural history is that it is part of something, evocative of something, extending something, that is at least as basic—the origins of popular culture. The architects understood this. Out of the 19th Century came several fundamentally new kinds of people, and several fundamentally new kinds of experiences. The celebrity, the fan, the champion, the spectator, the sight-seer, and the tourist. All these were *new*, then—and, in a great many ways, they are still new. The seeds of mass-circulation, of books and newspapers and magazines, were sown then, too. Cabarets and concert halls and dance halls began to attract general audiences. Culture became, for the first time, a commodity; its evidence, a consumer-ship matter. France, with England running close behind, fell all over itself, indulging in the exchange of sensations, diversions, ideas. This is really the precedent, if there is one, that Beaubourg must be acclaimed for building upon—not the precedent of the Gallery of Machines (1889), not the precedent of structural purity and direct material expression that came to the fore in the 1920s, not the raw, rakish edges of the so-called Brutalism of the 1950s (just), nor the let-it-all-hang-out predilections of Archigram. Such precedents may, indeed, be cited. But the most informative precedent is that of the enlarged experience of the public, chiming together, in the 30 years leading up to World War I. This process of popular interaction was accelerated after that, and, with the advent of mass-media, far beyond. Beaubourg, in every sense, is an extrapolation and countenance of this trend, and, as such, this trend has been celebrated with a coherence and cogency which make disdain of its strictly architectural and theoretical premises slightly silly.

The big escalator edges upward, across the west face of Beaubourg. Overlooking the busy public square, it is an automated animation of collective cultural consciousness, which may be a reason why it breaks down once in a while. The public square itself, filled with vendors and exhibits and a replica of Constantine Brancusi's studio—this sloping plaza, with small pedestrianized streets leading into it from

round about, is an exposition in itself, with all the sensory sustenance of the grand old boulevards.

On the eastern face, close by the noisy, bustling Rue du Renard, the grand verticals of the buildings servicing systems, also exposed on the outside, meet the sidewalk and the traffic with a tranquility that stops just short of truculence. Those ducts and pipes, which look like an assortment of diving gear, magically express the processes of mechanical intervention on behalf of public comfort and, finally, do not seem too close for comfort at all.

The inside of Beaubourg, with those lofty layers of space, is damnably "universal" in its flexibility and openness. Spatial "universality" is, of course, one of the monumental self-deceits of the modern movement, and here, especially in the spaces devoted to the museum of modern art, the sheer fluidity can be easily fumbled when separate exhibitions find themselves sloshing together in an ill-defined fashion. In this respect, the five major floors of Beaubourg, being above the major public forum-style area on the ground level, are more like the vast display floors of a merchandise mart and, right now neither the art nor the visitor seem to dwell upon the other. The ambiance is one of browsing. There is a sense of option, wading through these vast floors, but not, as yet, one of orientation, definition, or consolidation. Eventually, Beaubourg's curators must fix upon greater fixity. A loose fit can only be carried, or thrown, so far.

There is a spontaneity and simultaneity of popular interaction, with culture giving commerce a leg up, all around Beaubourg. And ironically this is what, after all the heckling these past years, has redeemed the architecture, making it a genial composition of the social and cultural forces swirling through the mind of France today. This is a building that history longed for, never got, and . . . well, a building that history hasn't gotten yet. Those pipes and ducts will be moving a lot, including, one can be sure, the pride of posterity in France's having had the gall to get them up there in the first place.

THE GEORGES POMPIDOU NATIONAL CENTER OF ART AND CULTURE, Paris, France. Architects: *Piano + Rogers.* Engineers: *Ove Arup and Partners.* Contractor: *GTM—Grands Travaux de Marseilles.*

The structure of the building called Beaubourg meets the structure of the neighborhood called Beaubourg, looking over the new public square, and west across Paris to the Eiffel Tower. The structural conviction and consistency of the architecture, a few cast-steel elements composing the complete fabric, is a counterpoint, but a uniquely clarifying one, to the low-scale density of the surrounding scene and, in the plaza below, to the spontaneous, simultaneous activities and events that have been drawing people in. Here (below) the joining of the lattice-like beams to the columns by way of the pin-like *gerberette* connectors frame a dynamic, not dispassionate, architectural regard for the social, cultural, and spiritual connections that are inherent in public access to the processes and products of creative effort—whether the encounter is with visual art, as in Beaubourg's multivalent museum, or with the repository of information, ideas, literature, images, and language skills in its library. This architecture delivers itself of the passions, preoccupations, and currents of France, opening the circuits between leisure and the intelligent uses of leisure.

The high public hall, internalizing the drama of Beaubourg's public square, also shows the masterful way in which spatial character, structural facts, and the building's ganglia of services have been synchronized (below). This two-level area contains a mezzanine for the Center of Industrial Design (right, top) and, on the opposite, southern edge of the hall, another for temporary exhibitions. Another, deeper layer of space is beneath this hall, stretching out under the public square, including, discernible in the far-left part of the picture below, a sunken forum-style space for exhibitions, assemblies, and assorted multi-media, multi-disciplinary happenings. A second major component is the Public Information Library (right, middle), housed on the first three of the five upper wide-span floors—the first truly open library in France. The top floor, along with all of the fourth and part of the third, is given over to the Museum of Modern Art. This topmost range includes a restaurant that overlooks one of several outside sculpture terraces (right, bottom), the building's structural armature and mechanical parts enfolding the public experience. Those nostril-like components, looming over the terrace, are air handlers.

The universality of space in Beaubourg has been attained by a necessarily bold, ubiquitous structural system that, at times, seems to repress the identity of the art works being shown. But curatorial skill is overcoming this. As in this double-level portion of the Museum of Modern Art (opposite), the works are composed in a lively, informative sequence, susceptible to viewing from many points of position (and seriousness). The art *of* Beaubourg, as much as that inside, is the richness of social and visual sensations (photos below) as the city is latched onto, enlivening the building itself.

CONCERT SHELL FOR A ROMAN RUIN

The ancient Roman theater in Caesarea, Israel shown before restoration (left) has been equipped with a new stage and an acoustical shell (below) for symphonic music, smaller musical groups and soloists. The shell is movable and by day is concealed within a revetment in a low hill nearby. This solution was in response to the demand by archaeologists that no elements foreign to the ancient building be allowed to destroy the romantic essence of the site. The design, by George C. Izenour, Professor of Theater Design and Technology, Director of the Electro-Mechanical Laboratory at the Yale School of Drama and noted theater consultant, is in his words the result of a "rare conjunction occurring in Caesarea among the forces of government, archaeology, architecture, engineering and the performing arts. A time span of two thousand years was telescoped into a project which brought together people of many different talents, nationalities and experience. Modern communications, air travel, technology, instrumentation and structural engineering all played a part and in the end were made common cause with the excavated ruin of an ancient theater building." In the article which follows, Professor Izenour not only describes the Caesarea Festival Theater's acoustical problem and its solution, but draws upon his vast knowledge of the history of theater design and performance to place this contemporary design within a broad cultural and technological context.

Paul Gross photos

The site and its history

Halfway between Tel Aviv and Haifa on the Palestinian shore of the eastern Mediterranean lies buried the ruin of one of the great maritime cities of the Roman Empire—Caesarea Judea. Founded by King Herod the Great and named by him in honor of Caesar Augustus, this site has been occupied, off and on, for over 3,000 years by Phoenicians, Jews, Romans, Byzantines, Norman French, Venetians, Arabs and Turks and other waves of peoples who have come and gone. In the first century before Christ, Herod built this great city with Roman engineering help. Fragments of its artificial harbor and masonry breakwater still remain after twenty centuries. Hard by this harbor is one of the ancient city's great buildings, a Roman theater excavated in 1958-60 by an Italian archaeological team headed by Professor Antonio Frova, Instituto Lombardo-Academia di Scienze e Lettere, Milano. In Biblical times it was from Caesarea that Pontius Pilate and a succession of Roman procurators administered Roman justice and ruled in the name of Caesar the nation of the Hebrews, and from which St. Paul embarked on the missionary journey that took him to Rome. A thousand years later it was in Caesarea that the Crusaders established a fortress-beachhead manned by the knights of St. John, but which fell before the onslaught of Islam. In our time it is in Caesarea that Pablo Casals, Alexander Schneider, Isaac Stern, Leonard Bernstein, Igor Stravinsky, Yehudi Menuhin, William Walton and others make music in the excavated ruin of this ancient theater before an audience of Israelis in the land of their forefathers. Caesarea has become the setting of one of few

attempts by the combined forces of modern archaeology, architecture and engineering to restore the ruin of an ancient theater building to suit the exacting requirements of the contemporary performing arts. This is by no means the first or only attempt. The Greek theater at Epidaurus in the Peloponnese has for many years been the site of a modern revival in the open-air of the drama of ancient Greece in a festival setting, and

the partially restored Roman theater of Herod Atticus in Athens has been used for summer performances of music and drama. The Roman Theater at Orange in southern France and others have been used as outdoor auditoria for a great variety of performance and related activities. That there have been problems, mostly acoustical, that have mitigated against achieving wholly successful results is understandable, and what makes the attempt at Caesarea unique is the recognition by the Israelis that in truth problems did exist. The problems are usually ignored.

The acoustical problem

First of all, modern music, drama, and opera, while in a sense descended from ancient forms, are in no way like them. The substance of the form and

the forces used for presentation are vastly different and even more important—the audience is different in its tradition, background, and conditioning. Modern audiences are used to enclosed theaters and concert halls which produce an acoustical result far different from that experienced in open air auditoria. The ancients as a general rule were not so conditioned. Some scholars have compared the drama of ancient Greece to the opera and music drama of our time, but this is at best conjecture. Certainly nothing akin to the symphony orchestra existed in ancient times and modern drama is vastly different from ancient drama. But from a practical point of view, with regard to seeing and hearing performance in an outdoor theater, the problem, at least in principle, was the same then as now. The Greek word *theatron*, from which is derived our word theater, means literally a place for seeing. Drama of the ancient Greeks developing from dithyrambic and epic poetry utilized to the full the sense of hearing. In the open-air auditorium the transmission of sound energy was dependent solely upon what could be carried along a path consisting of the straight line of sight from the actor on stage to the spectator in the audience.

Theories of Vitruvius

Acoustics are a difficult matter, as Vitruvius in his quaintly empirical treatise on architecture tells us. There is no doubt that acoustics presented as great a problem to the ancients as now, for why else would Vitruvius have so harped on the subject? Approximately 75 per cent of what he has to say about theater design is either directly or indirectly related to the subject of acoustics. And I do not believe

these observations were necessarily his own. He cites other sources, mostly of Greek origin. His treatise begins with a short introduction concerning site selection, which hints at a definition of satisfactory ambient acoustical conditions, he details how sight lines are derived, and so long as he sticks to Euclidean geometry he is on safe ground. But he proceeds to get involved in musical and pseudo-mathematical theory and the now infamous resonant sounding vessel theory of amplification, finally leaving earth for the stars, getting lost in astrology and music of the spheres. Is it any wonder that ever since, acoustics, in the lay mind, has conjured up associations with magic and witchcraft? His basic assumption concerning sight lines, however, is as correct today as it was then, and he makes a good case for seeing lines being also the basis for good hearing lines from a sound source located on stage to the spectators in the auditorium. But to the modern mind, conditioned by science, from this point on most of what he has to say is charming nonsense. Today, with the benefit of hindsight, it is easy to see why the ancients could go no further in understanding acoustics. It was their inability to make field measurements of even the simplest kind because basic instrumentation for the purpose did not exist. Nevertheless, they came close to identifying acoustics as an energy system, and we must give them credit for having the good sense at least to do as their senses directed. They were never guilty of permitting architectural conceits to transgress the essential functioning of the theater. The true explanation of how pressure stimuli worked for the seeing and hearing senses—that

151

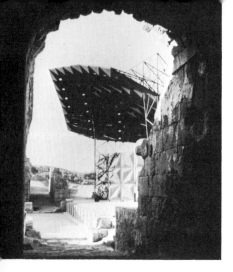

The canopy as seen by day (left) and by night (below) was built in Israel of weathering steel. A kite-shaped two-way space truss, its multi-faceted geometry consists of a series of small triangles which form larger triangles. The structural skeleton is fabricated of 1½- and 2-inch weathering steel pipe. The acoustical infill is fabricated of 18-gauge dampened weathering steel. The side wall units when folded and pivoted form either a modulated reflecting surface for music or a wing stage for dramatic presentation. The weight of the side walls is seven tons. The canopy, which includes its own lighting system, weighs 22 tons. The photographs show in juxtaposition two styles and systems of construction separated by 2,000 years—Roman stone masonry and contemporary tubular steel. Both are arch systems—the earlier spanning barely 12 ft, the later over 75 ft.

would one day be reduced to scientific reality as a train of waves and quanta—was 2,000 years in the future. In a more general sense it is the disparity between visual and aural sensation that has been, and in many ways still is, the problem central to theater design.

The search for a new approach

The first communication about the project at Caesarea was from Arnon Adar, the foremost Israeli stage and lighting designer, and an old friend of earlier times at Yale, who spelled out some of the problems being encountered. A subsequent directive with drawings and photographs from Yaacov Yannai, director for Israeli National Parks, indicated that symphonic music, smaller musical groups and soloists were the principal users and that all performances, due to extreme summer heat, were to be held in the cool of the evening under artificial light.

Both communications made no secret of an almost intolerable acoustical problem for listeners as well as performers, and aerial photographs revealed a nearby beach with pounding surf. A drawing marked up to show the prevailing winds revealed that they blew past the performer, whose back was to the beach, to the audience. From this information it was reasonable to deduce that windborne surf noise plus the effect of the wind itself was the principal problem and was responsible for a low signal-to-noise ratio. It was quite obvious that a shell structure that could collect, redirect and approximately double the sound energy over that presently experienced in the theater was in order. It is pointed out here that, contrary to popular belief, wind makes

for a difficult ambient acoustical condition in open air auditoria. In addition to carrying outside extraneous noises it creates noise as it blows past the ear lobes. There is on record a scholarly opinion developed in support of the theory that ancient theaters were situated so that the prevailing wind blew from the performer to the spectator, putting forth the belief that prevailing winds in the right direction were an aid to acoustics. Acoustical measurements made at these distances in theaters by myself tell otherwise, and this theory is nonsense.

The first design

An acoustical shell design based on simple ray diagramming was begun in 1966 without benefit of direct contact with the users or a visit to the site, using aerial photographs and drawings of archaeological remains as the only sources of information. These documents indicated the Roman stage to be almost a complete ruin, and a few photographs showing recent use indicated that the stage itself was not being used and performance had taken place in the orchestra, which had been temporarily floored over with wood. The audience was forced to do the best it could—seating itself on an incline of rubble which was an accurate description of the condition of the seat bank. Since the usual shallow Roman stage was, for all practical purposes, non-existent, I visualized some sort of tension structure suspended on cables over the orchestra as the most efficient and economical structural solution. The critical acoustical mass for efficient energy reflection in acoustical shells is of the order of two to three pounds per square foot, which in my experience is easily achieved by

16- 18-gauge dampened steel sheet.

The first design consisted of a fixed central steel mast from which was strung a network of cables fore and aft, with the cables over the ancient orchestra supporting the acoustical canopy and a modulated rear wall placed behind. There was never a thought of using material other than steel which for some years I have been using in the design of acoustical structures in multi-purpose buildings for the performing arts. It is well known that dampened steel reacts to an acoustical energy field in the same way as its equivalent mass of wood, masonry, hard plaster and other materials. I am not a believer in the old saw proclaiming that "sound is round and wood is good." After the initial study, resulting in the first design (below) was completed,

I was invited to Israel for a first-hand look at the site and a conference with the client.

It was obvious, though tacit, that to a man they were horrified at my suggestion that a mast be permanently placed at stage center and cables be dead-manned into the seat bank as the essential elements of the design. I was not then aware of a previous decision to restore and use the Roman stage instead of the orchestra as the performing area, quite as the Roman designer had initially intended, and a subsequent visit to the site quickly convinced me of the correctness of this decision. Also, between the time I began work on the design and my first coming to Israel, the decision

was made to restore the seating system with precast concrete panels of the same size and shape as the original masonry using rubble taken from the site as aggregate. This reconstruction made the audience at least as comfortable as its ancient counterpart. The work of restoring both stage and seatbank was well under way and, as a working committee, we were now ready to design in earnest. From the beginning, the department of antiquities people made the point that, no matter what acoustical and structural solution was eventually decided upon, the structure had to be movable because the archaeologists wanted to preserve as nearly as possible the excavated appearance of the site at all times when it was not in use for performance. For Caesarea, as an archaeological site and tourist attraction, this was a necessity. But on the other hand, the musicians complained bitterly and threatened not to ever again perform in the theater unless two essential requirements were met: first, provision to enable them to hear each other so they could play together; and second, just as important, provision for the audience to hear them without electro-acoustical help (amplification). To further complicate matters, it had been decided that in the future, works for the stage (opera, dance, and drama) would also be included in the program. This made it imperative that the acoustical solution for music be integrated with the stage as well.

A fresh start

To make a long story short, the tension structure was forthwith abandoned with no regrets and I returned home with clear directives on how to proceed, but not on how to solve the prob-

As the aerial photo (below) indicates,
the Roman stage instead of the orchestra
is being used as the performing area.
The seating system has been restored
with precast concrete panels
of the same size and shape
as the original masonry using rubble
taken from the site as aggregate.
The ancient masonry of the stage
and its environs has not been disturbed.
The canopy straddles the ruin.
The sidewalls pivot and fold
and when not in use the entire assembly is
tracked off stage right and hidden.
In this photograph 95 per cent
of the contemplated restoration work
is completed and the shell is
in playing position.

V. Braun

The canopy was fabricated, assembled and erected on the site. It terminates in three legs and as the details (below) indicate it runs on four wheels in two tracks, one set into the stage and the other in a drainage ditch behind the stage. The canopy space truss and front legs provide lateral arch action, the thrust of which is taken by a cable drawn taut between the legs at each wheel in the slotted stage track. Movement on and off the stage is effected by manual winches at each end of the track.

lem. Acoustical measurements taken at the site indicated only one practical approach, namely, to increase the signal-to-noise ratio by raising the energy delivered to the audience. Screening out the ambient noise would not be practical, is rarely if ever successful, and is usually impossible of attainment in outdoor auditoria.

The final solution

The fact that the structure had to be movable and retire to a position off the stage and out of sight was another problem high on the list of priorities, with the added restriction that the remaining ancient masonry of the stage and its environs was not to be disturbed. A number of schemes were hatched and abandoned until we evolved the idea of a canopy structured so as to straddle the ruin, mounted on flanged wheels which tracked off stage right for some 330 feet into a low hill adjacent to the original excavation. At my suggestion the hill was revetted for the purpose of hiding the canopy when it was not in playing position.

The canopy was built in Israel of weathering steel, exactly as designed. Structurally, it is a two-way space truss shaped like a great kite. The geometry consists of a series of small triangles which form larger triangles. The large center element is isosceles with small isosceles infill. The flanking arrays—right and left—are large right triangles with small right triangle infill. The skeleton is fabricated of 1½- and 2-inch weathering steel pipe with convex tetrahedra as the acoustical infill fabricated of 18-gauge dampened weathering steel. The canopy terminates in three legs, and runs on four wheels in two tracks, one set into the stage, the

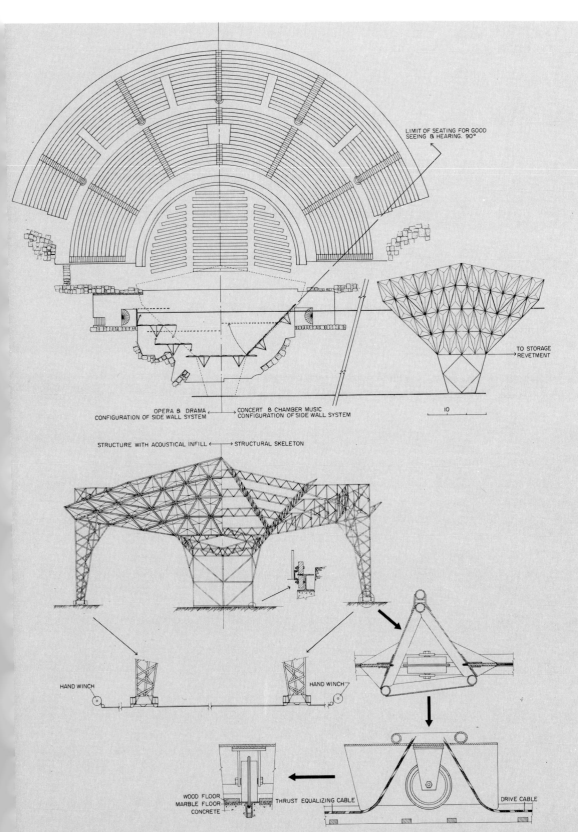

LIMIT OF SEATING FOR GOOD SEEING & HEARING. 90°

TO STORAGE REVETMENT

10

OPERA & DRAMA CONFIGURATION OF SIDE WALL SYSTEM ← → CONCERT & CHAMBER MUSIC CONFIGURATION OF SIDE WALL SYSTEM

STRUCTURE WITH ACOUSTICAL INFILL ← → STRUCTURAL SKELETON

HAND WINCH

HAND WINCH

WOOD FLOOR
MARBLE FLOOR
CONCRETE

THRUST EQUALIZING CABLE

DRIVE CABLE

The aerial photograph (below) shows clearly the canopy and the portion of the site which has been restored. The lines imposed upon the photograph (right) show the extent of the ancient Roman theater. "A" is the colonnaded lobby behind the stage house, "B" indicates the stage house, "C" shows the limits of the seat bank (auditorium) and "D" the wall which is part of a Byzantine fortification which incorporated the theater and was constructed ot masonry removed from the theater.

other in a drainage ditch behind the stage. The canopy space truss and front legs constitute lateral arch action, the thrust of which is taken by a cable drawn taut between the legs at each wheel in the slotted stage track. Movement off and on stage is effected by manual winches at each end of the track (one stage left and one located in the hillside revetment).

The shell is effectively closed from the edge of the canopy to the stage floor right, left and upstage by three-fold pivoting side wall units (six in total), which when folded and pivoted form either a modulated reflecting surface for music or a wing stage for dramatic presentation. They resemble the triangular pieces of machinery of the ancient Greek and Roman stage as described by Vitruvius. These are also fabricated of 1½ inch pipe and dampened 18-gauge weathering steel. The weight of the side walls total seven tons. The canopy weighs 22 tons, which includes its own lighting system, designed by Mr. Adar.

The results achieved during the first full seasons have been most gratifying. The musicians hear themselves without difficulty, and the acoustical field strength for music or voice, grounded in the audience has been doubled over previous experience without the shell. Quite apart from the fact that the structure works for modern means and contemporary audiences, there is one observation of interest to scholars of the ancient theater as well as to contemporary designers and acousticians concerned with a modern theater design. Scholars have long insisted that the low stage house of the Hellenistic theater represented a great acoustical improvement over the older Greek theater of the Classical Age. The claim is made that many of these stages were either built entirely of wood or had wood infill which then became a sounding board which was supposed to assist or to amplify the voices of the actors. These opinions were, I am certain, arrived at sans measurements and were aided and abetted by later seventeenth, eighteenth and nineteenth century theoreticians who had swallowed the bait cast by Vitruvius. It is interesting that the literature records no opinion concerning the acoustics of the ancient theater by a reputable scientist until almost the turn of the twentieth century. The first Caesarea festival provided the opportunity to test these phenomena.

The shell was supposed to be completed by mid summer for the first concert of the premier season, but due to the student riots and accompanying labor strike in France the sheet steel for the infilling of the shell was not delivered in Israel on time. But the show had to go on and at the last minute it was decided to use the side walls which compare favorably in height to the early Hellenistic stage and which were structurally complete but were not infilled. They were temporarily infilled with half-inch plywood and used without the canopy. The first concert was somewhat exceptional due to the large forces consisting of chorus, soloists and symphony orchestra. The acoustical ambient due to wind and surf was up to measured average and disappointment was complete. The field strength and the resulting signal to noise ratio showed virtually no improvement over that with no side walls, and electro-acoustic reinforcement had to be used. And because of the size of forces employed the musicians experienced greater than usual difficulty in keeping together. A concert of chamber music ten days later was somewhat more successful and got by with a minimum of electro-acoustical help but on this evening hardly a breath of air was stirring and there was no surf which bears out the previous contention of wind action. This condition of ambient quiet is similar to what I have measured in ancient theaters at inland sites like Aphrodisias in central Turkey and other isolated locations where low ambient is the rule, which demonstrates that above all else this is the essential criterion required to make an ancient theater work acoustically.

The missing steel arrived. There were now three weeks in which to finish fabrication and erect the moving canopy in time for the final concert of the season—the New York Philharmonic with Leonard Bernstein conducting Mahler's Fifth Symphony. The structure was finished barely twenty hours before the concert and I was asked if we would need the electro-acoustical reinforcement system. I answered in the negative and it was forthwith removed. We hoped for a repeat of a quiet night but it was not to be and the measured ambient was back up to its normal level of wind and surf. But by this time the preliminary measurements had given me enough confidence that I was certain of the result. The big moment had come and all of us were full of expectations and so it happened. The canopy made all the difference —and ray diagramming for the first reflections tells the whole story. The combination of steel side-walls and canopy in the sending end with the steep Roman seating system in the receiving end gave us the best of both worlds, modern and ancient. The direct sound and reflected sound arrive within about 30 milli-seconds for virtually all seats—even the ones high up and to the sides which in the reconstruction were purposely limited to the 90 degree spread of the shell. The instrumental balance was exceptional for outdoor auditoria. There are no foci for any of the more than 3,300 seats due to the non-curvilinear geometry of the shell. One other feature should be mentioned. Leo Beranek, Robert Newman and their colleagues have coined an excellent term for musical acoustics in the open air which they describe as "running loudness". This simply means that if there is enough energy and if it keeps coming, the sound is large and full bodied. The fact that there is no natural reverberation in the outdoors is because there are no natural return energy paths beyond the first reflections. It would be interesting in this instance, because of the excellent direct and first reflected energy, if reverberation were to be added by electro-acoustical enhancement. This enhancement should not be confused with electro-acoustical amplification, a necessity before the shell was built. If this should ever be accomplished we will have come full circle and provided for the first time in an ancient theater a reverberation system of the proper interface that works in lieu of the Vitruvian sounding vessels of legend.

THE FESTIVAL THEATER, Caesarea, Israel. Owner: *The Israeli Government Department of National Parks—Yaacov Yannai, director;* acoustical, structural and mechanical design: *George C. Izenour Associates, Inc.;* associate designer: *Arnon Adar, Tel Aviv, Israel;* construction engineer: *Gideon Kreiser;* supervising engineer for Department of National Parks: *David Kissin.*

NATIONAL AQUARIUM, OKINAWA

The lay of the land and the movement of the sun set the scale of this enchanting structural sequence, encrusting a narrow north-south site between a rocky shoreline and a steep, verdant rise. Seemingly of the sea, rather than just beside it, the Aquarium, the only permanent facility in a recent International Ocean Exposition, is a "path of shade," as Maki describes it, using two-level arcades as a sun- and windbreaker, thus determining the building's major expressive element and defining its processional nature.

The arcades, setting up an almost lyrical rhythm, are composed of concrete arches that express the dry-jointed juncture of precast three-hinged parts. This technique shortened construction time and, crucial to the area, did not require skilled labor to achieve an otherwise sophisticated configuration. Involving elements that act as a post-and-beam (two of them creating the three-hinged arch) and as floor or roof slabs, the system achieves maximum flexibility with minimum means. Nearly 300 post-and-beam elements and 150 of the floor slabs were used here, wrapping about the internalized spectator areas, framed in steel, while recurrently disclosing dramatic views of the natural environment.

The spectator areas inside show actual biological groupings within the world's biggest fish tanks. The first, 12 meters square and over two meters high, represents the Coral Sea, with some 6,000 fish, and shows life in shallower waters. Natural sunlight dapples in here from above, keeping the coral alive, and highlighting the sea-floor landscape in which most fish develop. The other tank, 12 by 27 meters and 3.5 meters high, represents the Japan Current, with some 8,000 fish, and shows life in deeper, outer waters. Including sharks and rays, these waters are kept deliberately still to simulate actual conditions. Thus these two tanks, being sizable semblances of the aqueous habitat, allow the tendencies and territoriality of the species to form.

Lining the tanks, which are viewed through expansive panels of frameless acrylic, are comfortable carpeted lounge areas, bathed in background music, where visitors can quietly contemplate the spectacle amidst subdued colors. These exhibits are a cause of reflection in a visual sense, too, as the corridors and lounges, with their lighting and finishes, pick up the evanescent play of light, water and marine life within the tanks and one is brought to wonder whether it wasn't the group biology of human beings that Maki was trying to display for the benefit of the fish. Visitors are further schooled by specific exhibits in the areas around the tanks, each concentrating on a particular species, set of interacting species, or pattern of biological and social behavior. This constant cross-reference between the comprehensive marine environment and the more specialized traits within it makes for an effective, accurate depiction, engenders a more fluid arrangement of spectator space, and

The National Aquarium on Okinawa is a processional enclosure whose scale is conditioned by the nature of the climate and the contours of its seaside site. From the entrance plaza (above, left foreground), two-level arcades, made of precast concrete, protect visitors from the bright sun and provide engaging views of the environment (left). At the north end of the complex, just downhill, is the Dolphin Theater (right), where visitors are seated beneath a huge arch-hung fish net.

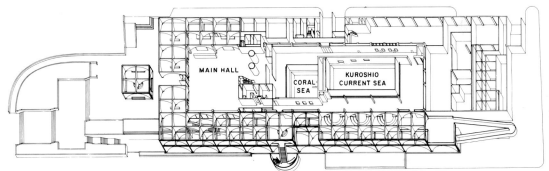

MAIN HALL

CORAL SEA

KUROSHIO CURRENT SEA

Photos courtesy of Maki and Associates

avoids the familar exhibition fallacy of people bunching together around repetitive little windows in order to get a glimpse of one fish or another taken out of its larger environmental context. In this design, the naturalness of that context, not the superclassification of curators, called the shots. What one experiences is an immersion in what is real—not an artificial rendition—to an extent that the displays have an almost surreal impact on the senses.

Outside and to the south of the Aquarium is a facility called Dolphin Land, which has two components. Okichan Hall is a small theater with live underwater shows and films dealing with the scientific aspects of these markedly intelligent large-brained dolphins. Whistling and clicking around hydrophones, their "conversation" is amplified, while those frequencies beyond our audible range are picked up on an oscillograph. Just downhill and adjacent is the separate Dolphin Theater, its stepped-up spectator section protected by a fish net canopy that is suspended from a simple bow-shaped arch. Here the shows are cast in high comic relief, what with high jumps, tail walks, and mid-air turns.

In the same sense that the design of the Aquarium and its exhibitions defer to the nature of marine life, the general scale and specific detailing of the structure itself are meant to evoke the characteristics of local custom and culture. The external wall surfaces are painted amber, much like the color used on many Okinawan houses. The rounded tile-covered handrails pick up designs of long local lineage. There are fierce lion statues guarding either side of the entrance plaza at the northern end of the complex where the play of arches and a bow-shaped roof, going back to the traditional use of such formal themes in native culture, intimates the arcaded walkways just beyond and confides the over-all character of the building composition even before one enters. Out of both climatic and cultural circumstances, then, the Aquarium is cadenced long and low on its site and, with its arcade, one knows right away how the building was made and, with the infernal summer sun, why the arcades run the way they do and what important function they perform.

Also telling is the way that the concrete and steel-framed internal structure enfolding the exhibitions also "reads" true. Tucked back under the precast concrete sections, brick surfaces, laid up over the lower portions of concrete and of a color that complements the amber of the outer arcade, tell the story of a function within that is sharply distinguished from the sun-shielding circulation function of the arcade itself. Articulating such opposites clearly, Maki reconciles them. The arches, without actually expressing internal function, provide a congruous, connective theme. A more discerning relationship between function and form is effectively established.

NATIONAL AQUARIUM, Marine Life Park, Okinawa. Client: *Ministry of Trade and Industry.* Architects: *Maki and Associates.* Engineers: *Kimura (structural); P.T. Morimura (mechanical).* Contractor: *JV— Kajima, Konoike, Tokyu, Sumitomo, Kumagaya, Zentaro.*

The interior exhibition and spectator areas, in contrast to the spritely, sun-shielding theme of the arched arcades outside, are muted and quiet. Lounge areas (above) are ranged repetitively opposite the large fish tanks (left) in which are housed true-to-life renditions of the actual habitat of shallow- and deep-water species. The major entranceway area (right) confides the arcaded character of the external form, while preserving and distinguishing the reinforced concrete and steel-framed vocabulary of the internal structure.

**A once-loved civic monument
on a prominent downtown site
restored to its former grandeur
by Chicago architects
Holabird & Root**

A once-loved civic monument on a prominent downtown site restored to its former grandeur by Chicago architects Holabird & Root

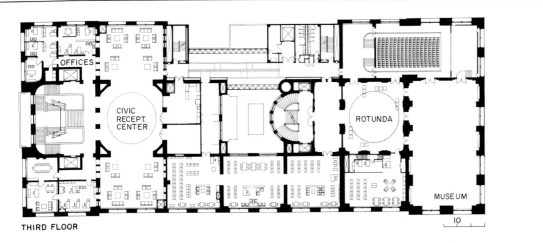

THIRD FLOOR

The Nineteenth Century's love of pomp, of ornament, of pageantry, of noble sentiment were all on display when the Chicago Public Library first opened its doors in 1897. The filagreed domes of Tiffany glass, the cartouches, the marble inscriptions, the huge spaces all combined to summarize an attitude toward civic building and civic pride. As the decades passed, however, the building began to suffer from serious neglect: ornaments began to crumble, surfaces collected veneers of soot and grime. Finally, in 1970, after proposals to modernize the structure were abandoned, demolition was suggested.

Eleanor Daley, the late mayor's wife, led a campaign to save the structure and before long an $11 million restoration program was officially inaugurated. Chicago architects Holabird & Root were commissioned to direct the restoration that included conversion of many former library spaces into areas for exhibit and display. By removing many towering bookstacks, long sweeps of space became possible and functional problems, which had plagued several generations of librarians, could also be attacked and solved. The largest task, however, was the restoration of neglected surfaces. Selected craftsmen from all over the country painstakingly cleaned and repaired the fine mosaics and restored the stained glass domes over the two rotundas, domes that had been covered over in the 1930s to forestall leaks.

What has emerged, after years of work, is splendid cultural space of a kind seldom affordable today and only achievable at all when people are willing to invest time, energy, and sympathy in their cultural past.

CHICAGO CULTURAL CENTER, Chicago, Illinois. Architects: *Holabird & Root—Gerrard Pook, partner-in-charge.* Contractor: *Paschen Construction Company.*

Reading rooms and work spaces both for the public and staff are now air conditioned in summer and heated in winter by a steam plant within the building.

The architects were determined to retain whatever they could of the Library's original detail and surface enrichment. New furnishings have been selected with care.

Casa Thomas Jefferson, Bi-National Cultural Center, Brasilia

It has been said that where there is no vision, there is a void. Brasilia conjures up both. A good place to go bananas over this pylon-studded polemic is on the upper tier of the rooftop amphitheater of Casa Thomas Jefferson, located in one of the city's more neighborly districts, and built by the USIA, always gung-ho for getting out good news, in collaboration with a local group called the Thomas Jefferson Cultural Council. Once not so hep about design, the USIA got out some good news here.

In contrast to the seething symbolism that one beholds from the rooftop, the Casa is a nice neat hit for humanism, with some of the spontaneity of a *favella* in Rio. A functional mix is contained within several two-level structures that are smartly scrunched together. Like iron filings, these fragments gravitate around a landscaped interior courtyard, a deliberately magnetic, unifying field of space with colorful flowers, exotic trees, and cooling pools of water.

At several points, the courtyard seeps out to the surrounding streets in the form of shoulder-squeezing, slit-like walks which, cut between the fragments at the far corners of the over-all composition, offer intriguing glimpses inside. Wider entranceways are positioned in the middle, but on either side of the courtyard, second level overhangs give a sense of intimacy as one comes upon the inner space, supplying a clear clue to the complex, yet cohesive nature of the architecture that edges it.

The functional fragments contain 20 classrooms and two language labs; offices for the school faculty, the USIS, and the Fulbright program; a 25,000-volume library, just inside from an angular terrace; and on the other end of the courtyard, just inside from a second terrace where receptions and performances are held, a two-story-high, skylit exhibition hall. Seen through the skylight, the rooftop tiers of the amphitheater edge upward, and beneath it is a 250-seat multi-use auditorium. Interpenetrating lines of sight pull the interior surfaces, done in white, bright plaster, into a spritely continuum. The reddish-pink stucco of the exterior, the hue of local clay, closes around this variegation—both a countenance of and a check upon the traits of complexity.

Embellished as the Casa is with sculpture, paintings, and crafts—part of a remarkable program of exhibits and lectures—its construction was deliberately kept simple: a reinforced concrete frame, with terra cotta infill walls, and poured floor slabs.

Local workmen felt at home from the start using local techniques, moving their families onto the site. The place is familial still.

CASA THOMAS JEFFERSON, Brasilia, Brazil. Owner: *Thomas Jefferson Bi-National Cultural Council.* Architect: *Mitchell/Giurgola Associates.* Associate Architects: *Alcides Rocha Miranda, Elvin MacKay Dubugras.* Engineers: *Robert Silman, Jose Parisi* (structural); *Flack & Kurtz, Andre Czajka* (mechanical/electrical). Contractor: *Coencisa, Brasilia.*

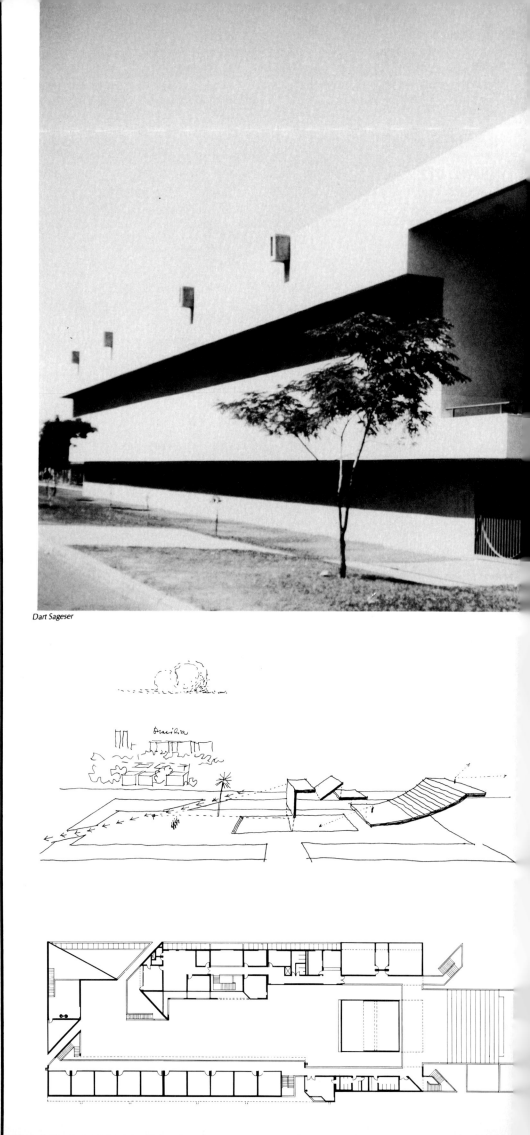

Dart Sageser

Romaldo Giurgola drawings

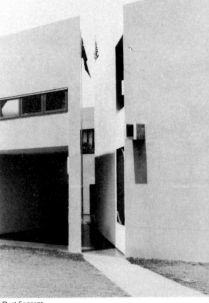

Dart Sageser

Unpretentious stucco walls set Casa Thomas Jefferson comfortably into its surrounding. Alternately low and narrow, entrances open into a lively, landscaped courtyard that discloses the functional fragments of the architectural composition. Entering one end of the courtyard, near the library (right) through slit-like walks, the exhibition hall is seen at the opposite end (bottom drawing, photo below right). Standing on the terrace in front of the hall (top photo, below), the plaster walls of the classroom and office wings ramble back toward the library. Inside the hall (top drawing), the rooftop amphitheater (bottom photo, below left) is glimpsed through a generous skylight.

Dart Sageser

Manu Sasoonian

Manu Sasoonian

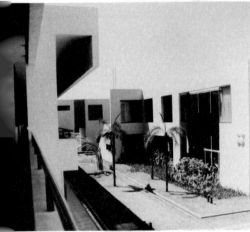

Dart Sageser

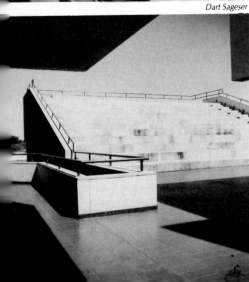

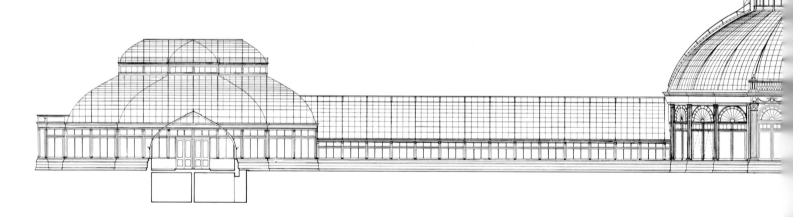

RE-CYCLING A GREAT CONSERVATORY AND ITS BOTANICAL GARDEN

The Conservatory of the New York Botanical Garden in the Bronx is a remarkable building begun in 1899. It was inspired by the Great Palm House at the Royal Botanic Gardens at Kew, England built between 1845 and 1847 by Decimus Burton in the Italian Renaissance style. Other precedents for its design were Sir Joseph Paxton's Crystal Palace built for the 1851 Great Exhibition in London. A building designed for the New York Exhibition of 1853 with a dome at its crossing might also have been a precedent. The Bronx Conservatory is believed to have been designed by William R. Cobb, architect for Lord & Burnham, then and now prominent manufacturers of greenhouses.

The photographs on this and the opposite page show the building as it appeared shortly after 1902. Although severely mutilated by insensitive restoration in 1938 and 1953 (see photographs on the next pages), it still possesses its great double dome and cupola, its cruciform corner pavilions and handsome apses.

The structure has now been extensively restored as part of an over-all scheme for the physical improvement of the entire garden. The work has been done done under the direction of architect Edward Larrabee Barnes and his associate, Alistair Bevington; and landscape architect Dan Kiley and his partner Peter

Ker Walker who restudied the garden.

The drawing above shows the restoration of the ornamentation on the central domed pavilion. The wings and cruciform pavilions remained unadorned (they lost their original filigree in the 1938 reconstruction and repair performed by the Department of Parks, and the cost of replacement is prohibitive). Two wooden vestibules which face the garden were restored to their 1902 appearance.

According to Siglinde Stern, project architect for the Conservatory recontruction, the work of restoration was exceedingly difficult because the original Lord & Burnham drawings could not be found. They were believed to

Photos courtesy of The New York Botanical Garden

The Conservatory, begun in 1899, was once richly ornamented, as the photos above and below, taken in 1902, indicate. As will be seen in the photographs on the next two pages, virtually all of this ornamentation has been destroyed partly by aging, but chiefly by blundering attempts to improve the building in 1938 and 1953. Because of limited funds, the current restoration included only repairs to the building's structural and mechanical system, replacement of broken glass and the reconstruction of the ornamentation of the central domed pavilion as shown in the drawing below. Two small vestibules facing the Conservatory terrace were also reconstructed. The interior partitions were restored to their original beauty.

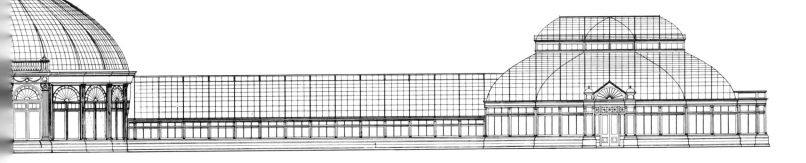

have been lost in a Parks Department cleanup in 1933. She resorted to measured drawings which were made in 1938 in preparation for that remodeling and used old photographs like the ones on these pages for detail sources and inspiration.

First priority was given to arresting the rapidly progressing deterioration of the building. Defective and corroded members of the steel superstructure were replaced. The glass skin and all its parts, such as the rafter bars and glazing bars, were replaced or repaired as required. The defective roof and sidewall ventilators were replaced or repaired. The exisiting

Courtesy of The New York Botanical Garden

John V.Y. Lee photos except as noted

steam heating system was replaced, the entire building rewired and new water supply piping and new floor drains installed.

The photographs above show the extent to which the building had been damaged by inept remodeling as well as decay and neglect. The south entrance to the central domed pavilion (directly above) which was perpetrated by the Parks Department in 1953 was removed, as was the brick wall and waterfall (also the work of the fifties) at what was once the north entrance (top right). The original cast iron facades and interior vestibules were reconstructed at these locations. The wood vestibules were altered in 1938 (opposite page, top) and the two of these which face the Conservatory terrace were restored to their original rather exotic appearance. (They never went very well with the Italian Renaissance facades of the central pavilion as can be seen in the photo overleaf, but their restoration summons forth the genial spirit of eclecticism which graced so many turn-of-the-century buildings designed for such passive pleasure.)

Badly damaged or missing were the wood and glass partitions which separate the various elements of the Conservatory. These were also reconstructed. The arched transoms in the central domed pavilion which were crudely simplified in the 1938 restoration (top left) were rebuilt with the delicate ornamentation of the original design.

As shocking as the mutilating additions was the present planting scheme for the Conservatory courtyard (above) and the terrace at the rear. These elements were restudied as part of the over-all master plan for the horticultural design and development of the grounds. The Conservatory courtyard became a site primarily devoted to the interests of city gardeners who garden in pots, tubs, boxes and other containers. Included were a wide variety of trees, shrubs and flowering plants, topiary and other trained specimens, as well as vegetable gardens to educate, stimulate and encourage

The central domed pavilion was left relatively intact (opposite page, top left) during the 1938 restoration, except for the arched transoms which were crudely simplified, but the vestibules were remodeled badly (right). This restoration, however, saved the building, for important structural and mechanical repairs were made at the time. The 1958 remodeling (opposite page, top right and below) was a total disaster. The terrace entrance to the conservatory was walled up and the wall became a back drop for an ill-conceived fountain. A "modernistic" entrance vestibule was applied to the courtyard side and clumps of bushes were planted to conceal the building's curves.

everyone interested in city garden methods and techniques.

The restoration also reflects the fact that the New York Botanical Garden is not exclusively an institution for botanical research, but, as Garden president Dr. Howard S. Irvin points out "is a great public amenity and a recreational resource for New Yorkers and visitors from all over the world." Until recently the Conservatory building had been a greenhouse for the plants which Dr. Irvin calls "the tough survivors"—those which were able to stand the overheating in its not-too-sensitive environment. The new improvements in climate control permit a far greater variety of plants

and greater flexibility in topical and seasonal exhibits. In its efforts to reach out to the people of the Bronx community whose brick and concrete neighborhoods offer little by way of trees and grass and where free amenities are limited, the Botanical Garden sees the Conservatory as a stage for special community-oriented events. At the same time, the restoration provides sufficient flexibility to serve the Garden's public audience which is extremely varied in its interests and knowledge.

While the restoration of the Conservatory has first priority, a new exhibition structure called the Plants and Man Building will eventually be constructed. Architect Barnes ex-

plains that as the Conservatory is oriented to horticulture, the Plants and Man Building will be directed to botany, ecology and other biological relationships between plants and man. According to the program developed by the Garden, it will include "special examples of plant relationships such as mimicry, plants that grow on other plants, parasitism, insectivorous plants, plant adaptations, and interrelationships between certain plants and animals including, of course, mankind."

As described by Barnes, the Plants and Man Building will be a totally new kind of glass structure. It is composed of hexagonal modules, roughly 45 ft across, that may be

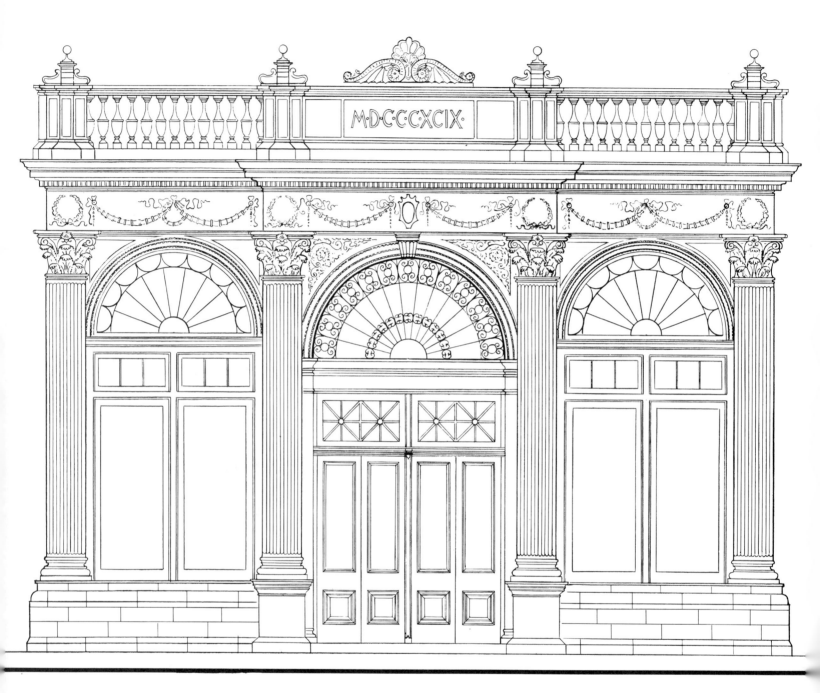

grouped together vertically or horizontally to crate a plant system environment of any desired size. The walls of these chambers may expand vertically to accommodate the growth of trees. Each plant system environment would have its own indigenous climate (see overleaf).

The building in plan forms a handsome forecourt which leads to the building entrance and to the garden beyond. This undulating glass structure will not be a closed prismatic form. Infinitely flexible, it will interlock the plants within it with the surrounding landscape. As Barnes points out, the clustering of hexagonal modules has many parallels in nature: the honeycomb, the quartz crystal, the

microscopic plant structure itself. The hexagon, unlike the octagon and more elaborate geometric shapes, is a nesting form that can be combined simply and repetitively for growth in six directions. Like a beehive, the Plants and Man Building in the years ahead can add new modules as programs change and develop. High and low modules can nest side by side in endless variety.

The supporting structure will be a system of slender pipe columns, tubular beams and diagonal tension rods. The hexagonal roof of each module will slope to a central gutter and internal downspout.

Both the restored Conservatory and the

projected Plants and Man Building are the key display areas in a land use plan which will greatly improve the Garden's usefulness as a public educational and recreational resource. In the summertime the Garden serves as one big back yard for people within walking distance in the Bronx. Picnic tables are provided. According to Dr. Irwin, the Garden has a very high standard of maintenance and this in turn encourages its users not to litter or vandalize. In recent years there has been little conflict between the need to protect the Garden and its buildings and plantings and the need to make it free to all as a green oasis in the city and the reasons for that happy truth might well be care-

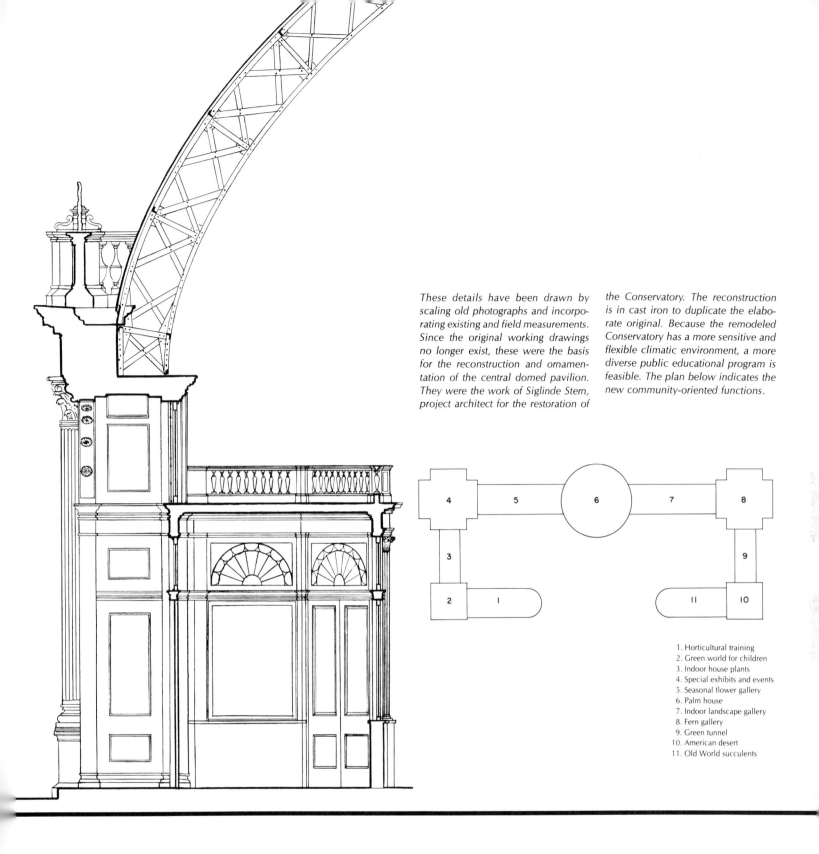

These details have been drawn by scaling old photographs and incorporating existing and field measurements. Since the original working drawings no longer exist, these were the basis for the reconstruction and ornamentation of the central domed pavilion. They were the work of Siglinde Stern, project architect for the restoration of the Conservatory. The reconstruction is in cast iron to duplicate the elaborate original. Because the remodeled Conservatory has a more sensitive and flexible climatic environment, a more diverse public educational program is feasible. The plan below indicates the new community-oriented functions.

1. Horticultural training
2. Green world for children
3. Indoor house plants
4. Special exhibits and events
5. Seasonal flower gallery
6. Palm house
7. Indoor landscape gallery
8. Fern gallery
9. Green tunnel
10. American desert
11. Old World succulents

fully studied by other park planners.

The master land use plan for the 250-acre Garden, prepared by architect Barnes with landscape architect Kiley, takes measures to preserve those undeveloped areas best suited as a nature preserve, while making the Conservatory and the projected Plants and Man Building and their surrounding courts and terraces more accessible to the public.

As the present and future land use plan (overleaf) indicate, the boundaries of the Garden are redefined. Fencing, pedestrian gateways and major entrances are better related to the most frequently visited areas. A new main entrance and bus and auto drop-off has been

designed (see model photograph, overleaf) which, according to Barnes, has been inspired by the work of Frederick Law Olmsted. As occurs in a number of locations in Central Park, pedestrians will enter a grotto-like tunnel which burrows through a mound and opens into a broad and verdant landscape. The tunnel will heighten the experience of contrast between the world of the Garden and the world of the Bronx. Opening off the tunnel will be sky-lit grotto shaped spaces which will contain a plant and book store, and orientation center, toilets and a guard office.

Within the Garden all unnecessary roads will be eliminated and private cars will be re-

stricted to the peripheral road which gives access to the Conservatory and the Plants and Man Building. This will enhance the attractiveness of the Garden immeasurably, attract bicyclists, encourage people to walk, and reduce air pollution. To enable people to visit the more remote parts of the Garden, Barnes and Kiley propose the use of small electric buses which will follow a peripheral route that will circumscribe the outlying natural areas of the Garden and interconnect them with the Conservatory and the Plants and Man Building. To complete this admirable circulation plan, an aerial tramway has been proposed to link the Garden with the Bronx Zoo.

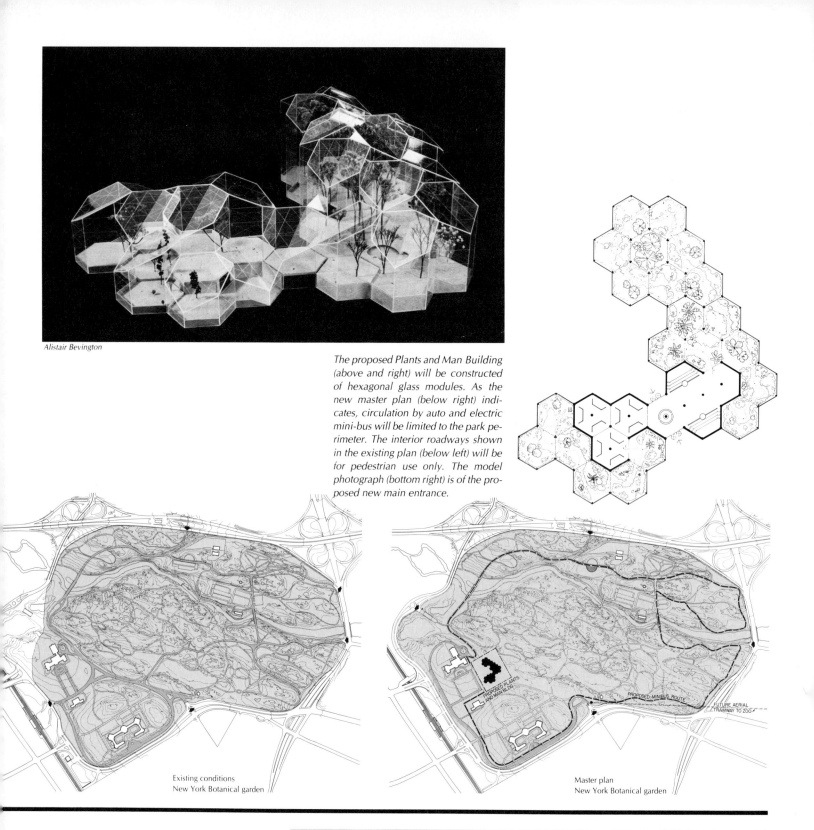

Alistair Bevington

The proposed Plants and Man Building (above and right) will be constructed of hexagonal glass modules. As the new master plan (below right) indicates, circulation by auto and electric mini-bus will be limited to the park perimeter. The interior roadways shown in the existing plan (below left) will be for pedestrian use only. The model photograph (bottom right) is of the proposed new main entrance.

Existing conditions
New York Botanical garden

Master plan
New York Botanical garden

NEW YORK BOTANICAL GARDEN RESTORATION, Bronx, N.Y. Master plan architect: *Edward Larrabee Barnes—associate-in-charge: Alistair Bevington, project architect: David Arnold.* Landscape architect: *Dan Kiley & Partners—partner-in-charge: Peter Ker Walker.* Conservatory restoration architect: *Edward Larrabee Barnes—project architect: Siglinde Stern.* Consultants: *Weidinger Associates* (structural); *Arthur A. Edwards* (mechanical and electrical); *Billie S. Fritz* (industrial archeologist). Plants and Man Building architect: *Edward Larrabee Barnes—associate-in-charge: Alistair Bevington, project architect: David Arnold.* Consultants: *Weidlinger Associates* (structural); *Lehr Associates* (mechanical and electrical).

John V. Y. Lee

Savannah Area Chamber of Commerce and Visitors' Center

Completed in 1876, Savannah's railroad station had been totally unused for five years when the local chamber of commerce leased the facility from the city for their own offices and a visitors' center. It has been renewed by architects Gunn & Meyerhoff. Recently, Savannah has enjoyed an enormous increase in tourists, spurred on by a pleasant ambiance and one of the richest architectural heritages in the country. (Gunn & Meyerjoff are adding to this ambiance with a Federally-funded project to turn the city's riverfront into a park.) The consequent need for a central source of information (and promotion) was acute, and the most appropriate location was logically one of the city's early gateways, its railroad station.

In this just completed project, the architects have reinforced the original design by eliminating latter-day additions. Even the original windows were re-used. In the former waiting room—now the active visitors' center (photo, top), the double arch, which appears to lack a central support, "was probably always that way": The configuration covers the apex of an inverted triangular truss. Paint colors approximate the original. Air-handling ducts (as well as the lines of all of the mechanical services) were "snaked-through" existing cavities between finishes and structure. The process helps account for a relatively high construction cost for the area of $26 per square foot in 1975, but the cost is low for the qualities of the space obtained. (On a cubic-foot basis, the rehabilitation cost $1.70).

Robert Gunn is amused by the newness of the re-use concept in much of the rest of the country: "In Savannah we have always done this."

NEW OFFICES FOR SAVANNAH AREA CHAMBER OF COM-MERCE & VISITORS' CENTER. Owner: *Savannah Area Chamber of Commerce*. Architects: *Gunn & Meyerhoff*. Engineers: *William Hunter Saussy, Jr.* (structural); *White, Hobbs & McClellan* (mechanical); *J.A.M. Maddox* (electrical). Consultants: *Jane Furchgott, Rosolio's Inc.* (interiors). General contractor: *Atley Company.*

CHAPTER FIVE

MULTI-USE FACILITIES:
CIVIC CENTERS AND BUILDINGS WITH ALL TYPES OF FLEXIBLE USES

Almost as disparate in character as those projects shown in the chapter on cultural pursuits, the buildings in this chapter, at this stage in their development, are by definition different from one another. A relatively new type of construction for governments, multi-use buildings can combine various functions in endless non-formulated ways that fit the needs of the moment and the locale. Even the governments' concepts of what such a construction should accomplish vary radically from project to project.

Accordingly the examples in this chapter range in size from the large and sprawling Fairfield, California Civic Center designed by architects Robert Wayne Hawley & Associates to New York City's tiny Tompkins Park Recreational and Cultural Center by architects Hoberman & Wasserman. They range in character from the suburban Belmont, California Regional Center by architects Gantt/Huberman Associates to the big urban Onondaga County, New York Civic Center by architects McAffee, Malo/Lebensold, Affleck, Nichol. And they include a partially re-used group of urban buildings, the Pilot Center in Cincinnati by architects Woolen Associates. Their uses can include everything from theaters and gymnasiums to offices—sometimes in the same spaces.

As explained in the preface to this book, the projects in this chapter fall into two categories. The first is the more revolutionary, as it allows the same spaces to be used for different purposes with obvious savings in construction cost. The second more established, but still new, category of multi-use projects are civic centers—as opposed to government centers—which combine various functions in individual spaces or buildings on one campus. While the first-cost advantages obviously are greater with the former type, there are certainly first-cost advantages in the simultaneous construction of the buildings in civic centers. And there are administrative and communications savings as well.

Of the buildings (or groups thereof) on the following pages, architects Ciardullo Ehmann's South Paterson, New Jersey Library Community Center, and the Belmont Regional Center (both single buildings with multi-use spaces) best demonstrate the concept of housing more than one activity within the same spaces. And architects Gonzales Associates' Scottsdale Civic Center (also an interesting expression of local character), and the Fairfield Civic Center, might be most typical of grouped functions. But whether a grouping of functions in different spaces or a grouping in the same spaces, the multi-use projects seem destined to make up a good part of what will be built in the immediate future by Federal, state and local governments across the nation.

TOMPKINS PARK

While the New York City Board of Estimate had appropriated monies for a community center for the aged within an existing green-space, a Parks Department program (designed to make its new facilities responsive to the users) allowed an expansion of purpose because of discussions between community groups, the city and the architects. Local performing-arts groups, other cultural organizations, social functions and community meetings also needed accommodation and the building that emerged is a cultural and recreational center for users of all ages. While architects Hoberman & Wasserman involved themselves in the discussions with the city on behalf of the local residents, they would not describe the activist role as an easy one.

The original plan for this two-square-block area was designed by Fredrick Law Olmstead in the late nineteenth century, and—until recently—the park was surrounded by pleasant and substantial townhouses of the same era. The type of inhabitants has changed in the Bedford-Stuyvesant district, and local government is in the process of massive construction of new housing intended to eliminate the buildings associated with the present poverty—if not the cause.

When the architects received their commission, little of the original park as planned by Olmstead remained, and as it was designed for promenading it did not fit current community needs. Still, the building was placed to emphasize the original plan's axis, existing radial-walks were retained and a new fence, cutting off the western half, was eliminated. A playground, designed by Vollmer Associates, was a later-day addition and was incorporated in the new site plan.

The final program for the building called for about 12,000 square feet of enclosed space plus an outdoor amphitheater. In order to reduce the potential impact of a large building-volume on the neighborhood's badly needed green space, the architects buried more than half of that volume under the grade and sloped the outdoor areas at the two ends down to the depressed floor levels. One slope accommodates the concrete benches of the amphitheater. The depressed area at the other end of the building provides an exit from the indoor theater at the lowest level, access to the toilets (placed for both park and building users) and an outdoor lobby during performances. The visible building mass was fragmented by a courtyard separating the various elements and transparency was created by the use of large lights of shatterproof plastic.

The poured-in-place concrete walls were formed with depressed vertical-ribs to provide texture and make the surfaces less attractive to graffiti artists. The latter function has been only been only partially successful despite daily cleanings and an applied chemical-surfacing. "There is something just too attractive about a concrete wall," says architect Hoberman. The total construction cost was $1,500,000 including extensive site work in 1974.

TOMPKINS PARK RECREATIONAL AND CULTURAL CENTER, New York, New York. Owners: *Parks, Recreation and Cultural Affairs Administration.* Architects: *Hoberman & Wasserman—job captain: Andrew Freireich.* Engineers: *Finley & Madison Associates* (structural); *Arthur L. Zigas & Associates* (mechanical/electrical). Cost consultant: *John Meadows.* General contractor: *Petracca & Sons, Inc.*

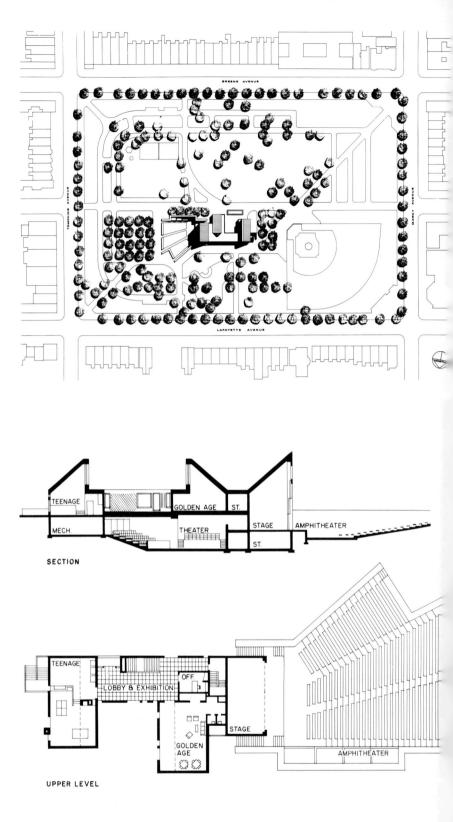

SECTION

UPPER LEVEL

LOWER LEVEL

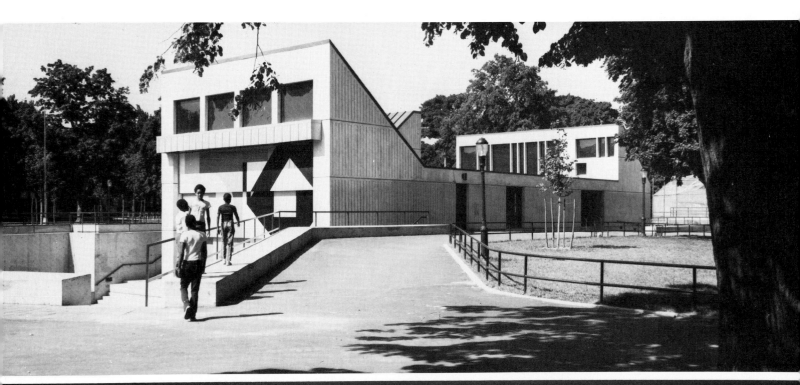

Norman Hoberman photos

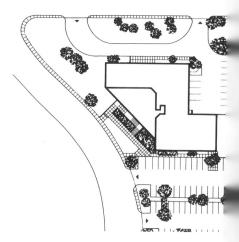

BELMONT REGIONAL CENTER

Gordon H. Schenck, Jr. photos

This building is a 25,000-square-foot neighborhood center in Charlotte, North Carolina, and its facilities include a day care service, a branch of the Charlotte Public Library, office space (designed to be flexible) for various social-service agencies including the county health department, a multi-purpose auditorium, classrooms, and meeting rooms. Outside, the day care facility has an enclosed play yard, and there is also extensive parking space on the site and drop-off and pick-up areas for busses and cars.

The site (see plan on the left) is in the shape of a trapezoid, and it slopes downward approximately 35 feet from its highest point to the small creek (which is at the bottom of the

plan). The architects decided that the building should be multi-level, and it should be located near the highest point on the site. Parking is located nearer the creek, and partially within its flood plain (large photograph above).

The main entrance to the building (photographs opposite) faces the main street and the passing traffic, thus announcing itself to passer-by, and also being accessible for entry from the adjacent parking lot. A secondary entrance, with convenient drop-off and pick-up points for busses and cars, is located off the secondary street (at the top of the adjacent site plan, and shown in the large photograph on the following page).

The lowest level of the Belmont Regional

Center houses the day care facility, which has its own entrance from the parking lot (extreme right of the three plans on the opposite page). The main floor of the building (center plan opposite) contains all of the social-service and educational facilities, which are grouped around the public lobby, shown in the photograph on the opposite page. Circulation through the lobby is accomplished by ramps, one of which can be seen in the background of the photograph opposite, behind the receptionist, who from her central position has visual control of the entire area.

The upper, or mezzanine, floor of the building houses the administrative offices for the center; above it, clerestory windows allow sunlight to flood into this area and into the lobby below.

The structural system for the building consists of one-way poured-in-place concrete slabs for the upper floors, and concrete columns, beams, and slabs on grade. The exterior walls are of red brick on block, with exposed concrete spandrel beams. The windows are bronze tinted glass which are housed in bronze anodized frames.

BELMONT REGIONAL CENTER, Charlotte, North Carolina. Architects: *Gantt/Huberman Associates— project architect: Scott Garner*. Engineers: *Frank B. Hicks* (structural); *McKnight Engineers, Inc.* (mechanical); *Ben Weinreb, P.E.* (electrical). General contractor: *Gates Construction Company*.

Gordon H. Schenck, Jr. photos

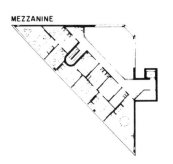

MEZZANINE

MAIN FLOOR

N

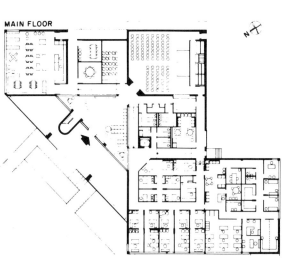

10

LOWER FLOOR

Nathaniel Lieberman

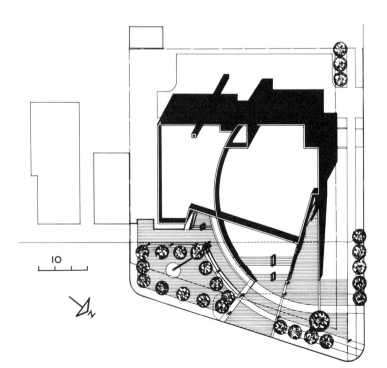

10

THE SOUTH PATERSON LIBRARY IS REALLY A MULTIPLE-USE COMMUNITY CENTER

The pressure of heavy usage on a former storefront facility caused t
city of Paterson, New Jersey, to build the new library shown here. Bu
the current spirit of cost consciousness, the city really wanted a comple
around-the-clock neighborhood center within the planned walls: poli
community relations offices, ambulance service facilities, commur
meeting spaces (including facilities for an elderly day care program)—a
of course books and audio-visual equipment.

To overcome the obvious problems of guarding books in a qu
place for reading—while all of the other proposed activities were taki
place—Ciardullo Ehmann separated the strictly library-related functic
onto the second floor, and the multi-use spaces onto the lower floor.
curved wall, which cuts through the building, defines traffic patterns
the upper and lower levels without emphasizing the importance
either—or making the building appear cut in two.

Indeed, perhaps the most interesting aspect of the planning (besic
the combination of uses) is the way in which the building recogniz
both its dual role and relation to the neighborhood in terms of massir
The main entrances face a busy commercial street on which the sm
paved and landscaped forecourt offers a welcome relief. The court w
created by closing a through street, and connecting the building's s

John McNanie

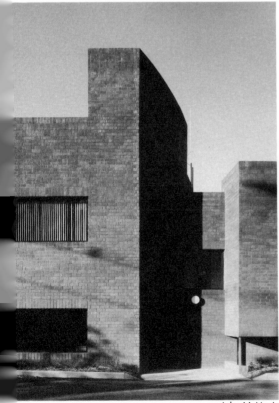

John McNanie   Nathaniel Lieberman

Nathaniel Lieberman

with what was formerly a small triangular park. The front of the building has been angled to relate to the main street, except for a projecting element on one side that continues the visual rhythm of the smaller-scaled adjacent structures immediately to the south. Much of the actual volume of the building is concealed below grade—especially on the front, where the forecourt rises to meet a point on the facade that is halfway between the two floors. An entrance for the ambulance garage is incorporated as part of the sculptural volume (see photo of side view, previous page).

The construction cost was $555,000 in 1978, including the cost of the forecourt. The structure is a combination of masonry bearing walls and round steel columns, which support steel beams and lightweight steel joists. The floors and roof are metal decking, and the cladding is brick which was chosen to fit into the surrounding structures and the community.

SOUTH PATERSON LIBRARY COMMUNITY CENTER,Paterson, New Jersey. Owner: *City of Paterson.* Architects: *Ciardullo Ehmann—project architect: Paul Spears.* Engineers: *Environmental Engineering (soils); George Deng (mechanical/electrical).* General contractor: *Franklin Universal Building Corporation.*

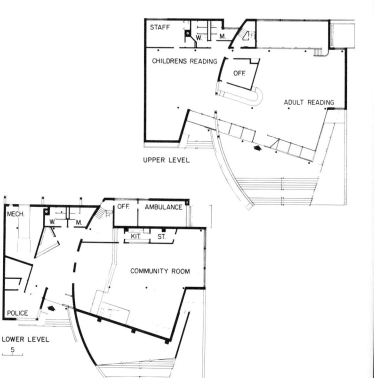

The lower-level community room gains light through a glazed slot facing the forecourt (photo, overleaf). The upper-level library is divided into a children's section and an adult reading room (photos this page). The reading room gains views of passing activity on the adjacent main street through large glass windows on the front of the building. These views are enhanced by raising the rear of the reading room, which also defines more intimate areas.

A LONG-AWAITED WELL-RESPECTED COMMUNITY CENTER

It took nine years for residents of New York City's Twin Parks area to receive the much-requested Webster Community Center, at right, because of administrative delays. Below, Kathleen Kelly, former manager of Twin Parks' scattered housing development for the New York State Urban Development Corporation (UDC), tells how Smotrich and Platt Architects, despite bureaucratic difficulties, created a beautifully functional structure well adapted to its surroundings and clearly enjoyed and respected by the people who use it.

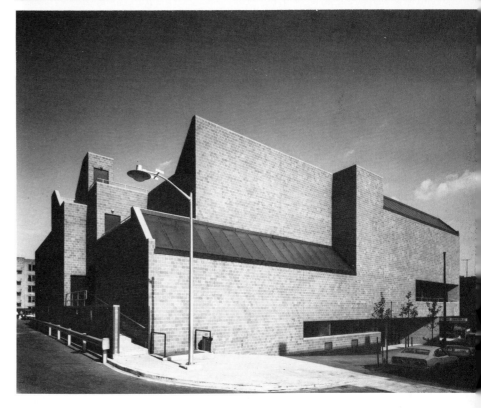

In the busy entrance to the Webster Avenue Youth Center in New York City's borough of the Bronx is a plaque bearing the names of the dozens of people connected with the Center's long history. The architects, David Smotrich and Charles Platt, stress that the plaque names people who helped, as well as hindered, the Center's development during the past decade.

Listed are John Ryan and other members of the local Police Athletic League who first pressed for the Center in the mid-sixties. They drew up the program for the Center eventually approved by the City and acted as Smotrich and Platt's clients. Because of their efforts and to honor a popular patrolman, the Center was officially named the Police Athletic League-Patrolman Andrew F. Giannone-Webster Community Center.

T'ing C. Pei, who shepherded the Center through most of its trials while working first for the New York City Human Resources Administration and then for the New York State Urban Development Corporation, is remembered on the plaque. He convinced the City that building a new facility would be less expensive than converting the old Metro Theater, which then occupied the site. Mr. Pei, fearing that the City's public works department would have legal and administrative difficulties in completing this innovative project, persuaded UDC to take it on as a turnkey to the City.

The names of several New York City Bureau of the Budget officials appear on the plaque. In spite of the City's public policy in support of the Center and in spite of the long-held expectations of the Webster Avenue community, these men required 18 months to examine three drafts of a working agreement between UDC and the City before finally approving one. They took seven months to review and approve schematic plans for the 30,000-square-foot facility and 16 months to review and approve preliminary working drawings.

Included on the plaque is the name of the Housing Authority official who responded to the architect's desire to coordinate site planning with the adjacent public housing project by saying, "Mr. Platt, nobody cares about these things, except maybe an architect once in a while. Certainly not the people who live in them."

Sharon Keilin resolved the labyrinthine problems of equipping the Center and is remembered on the plaque.

As is E.W. Howell, general contractor, who took responsibility for the building's safety for a year after its completion while the Bureau of

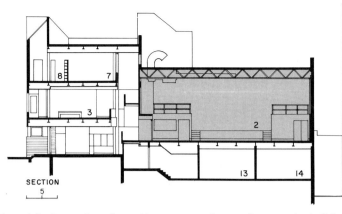

SECTION
5

Two of the impressions the architects wished conveyed through the Webster Center design were expressed articulation and community space. At far left, the Center's facades were defined by its interior spaces and skylights, giving the steel and brick structure heightened visibility when viewed against a backdrop of older, more conventional buildings. The second floor loggia ties the Center to the community and to its site. The Center's largest activity room is the gym (below) which occupies two floors on the building's north side while the smaller activity rooms occupy the south side (see floor plans at left and section above). The curtained stage can be seen at the rear of the gym below. Above, the interrelationship between the building's two parts is shown in the section where the floors meet at half levels along the main circulation corridors. As the architects claim, something is happening at each level along the staircase.

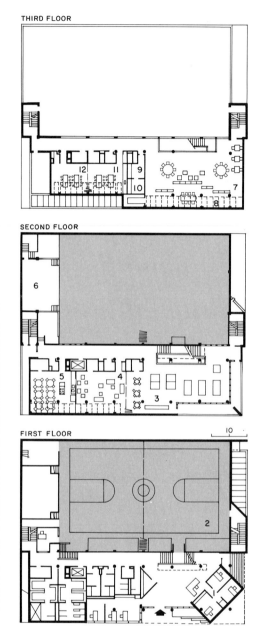

THIRD FLOOR

SECOND FLOOR

FIRST FLOOR

the Budget tried to decide which agency would run it.

Father Mario Zicarelli, the driving force behind much of the improvements in housing and education in this agglomeration of neighborhoods known as Twin Parks, is also remembered on the plaque. Just before the schematic design for the Center was presented to the City, he commented, "It's too simple. They'll never understand it."

And simple it is.

The site for this community recreation center is a cramped corner property at the intersection of two main routes of neighborhood traffic: north-south along Webster Avenue and east-west along dead-ended Ford Street and an important pedestrian easement through the Housing Authority project. The dual main entrance to the Center recognizes this corner and provides interior and exterior gathering and milling places. (The Housing Authority's plans to make this small section of Ford Street a play street were abandoned while the Center was under construction.)

While the building's program called for it to express a welcome to the community, the City severely restricted the use of windows and other openings onto the street. To overcome this conflict, skylights and a second floor loggia overlooking the street corner were incorporated, creating a feeling of openness, bringing in natural light and connecting the Center to the community. The western side of the building and the roof were given special consideration and painted in some areas to give the Housing Authority occupants a pleasant and interesting view.

A gym takes up the whole north side of the tiny site. The other half of the building is a three-story loft-like structure capable of being divided into smaller activity rooms. All the Center's circulation and services are situated between the two parts of the building staggered at half levels between the floors. A few rooms requiring special equipment are located in a partial basement, taking advantage of the site's natural slope and allowing them to be closed off when not in use.

On a visit during a recent school day, the dual corner entrance (steps on Webster Avenue and a ramp for the handicapped on Ford Street, see photo above) and the second-story porch and high sloping windows on the second and third stories, provided a sense of welcome despite the almost total absence of standard windows. The building's outward form follows the shape of its interior spaces to present an

articulated mass of projected ''edges'' that stand out in sharp contrast to the flat and regular surfaces of old-law tenements and new public housing next door. The Center is obviously a special place.

Inside, soon after school had let out, the spacious lobby was being used just as Smotrich and Platt had intended—as a general gathering place, almost as an extension of the street outside, where people going to and from the Center stopped to chat in pairs or small groups. Chairs were still stacked near one of the entrances, left over from a community function the night before. A senior citizens' arts and crafts group was at work at tables set up in the lobby, obviously enjoying the hubbub of youngsters moving through the area to and from the gym and the director's office which is located, for security and convenience, nearby.

Two young men were recruited from the general activity to give a tour through the now five-year-old building. In the gym, which is half a level above the lobby, several groups of children were practicing basketball. The tour guides noted that the platform at the west end of the gym had been used for a play just the week before.

Walking up the broad and only partially enclosed central staircase (there are also two enclosed fire stairs at the east and west ends of the Center) to the second story game rooms, sunshine from a clerestory window in the stairwell and from the skylights on the upper floors was obvious and welcome. Overzealous pool shooters playing at the head of the stairs apparently caused the only instance of broken glass at the Center so far—in the floor-to-ceiling windows looking out on the corner

porch. A fully equipped kitchen, used for domestic science classes as well as feeding special gatherings, is on this floor. An adjacent lounge, originally intended to accommodate a senor citizens' hot meal program, can be separated from the pool room and itself further subdivided by folding walls.

Noise from the first floor activities was only partially diminished here, but on the third floor where the library, chess tables and art rooms are located, near-quiet reigned. Here as on the second floor, the skylight-like windows face south, except in the art rooms where they face north.

Even down in the basement, the electronics, carpentry and ceramics shops were all lit by sunlight from a broad screened porch at the same level, which also serves as an outdoor work area in good weather. The only major

Typifying the Center's concept of community space is this open staircase, shown from the first floor lobby at left and across the second floor below. It is the major space associated with the linear spine of circulation and serves to link the building's two segments. The staircase is itself a vertical column of space extending upward and touching each floor. In keeping with this pattern of open freedom, the structural system forms spaces that surround the white columns, as seen in the right photo, rather than incorporating them into the spaces. Light filters to the stairs from the floors and skylights above. Portions of the large activity room where the pool tables are located can be seen at left below.

activity room, aside from the gym, which does not have natural light is another large basement room outfitted for classes in the martial arts and dance (complete with mirror and dancers' practice barre.)

Materials and furnishings throughout the building are absolutely basic, chosen for durability whenever possible, and for an optimum compromise between durability and initial cost the rest of the time. Smotrich and Platt's careful attention to costs contributed to a $30,000 savings in the Center's construction budget, a very substantial saving considering that it came during the 1973-74 period of greatest inflation in construction costs.

Although the Center now bears signs of its constant use, it is still as attractive as it was on the day of its official opening and dedication in 1975. There is no grafitti whatever on

the inside of the building and very little on the outside. A story repeated among the Police Athletic League may explain why the building is relatively unmarred. PAL members, who had established a good relationship with young people in the area, report that one day during the year the building sat completed but empty, a bit of graffitti appeared on the wall. Because they liked the Center and knew that it would one day belong to them, the youngsters themselves found the vandals and made them remove the markings. ''That's a nice thing for an architect to hear,'' Platt said.

The respect the youth have for Webster Center is again reflected in how much they utilize its facilities. On a typical summer day, 1000 visit the Center. Even during the school year, hundreds of youngsters and adults are in and out from morning 'til night, playing, relax-

ing, pursuing hobbies, exchanging the ideas of youth everywhere.

And there is only a modest plastic plaque with a jumble of names in the lobby to remind users of those nine incredible years from 1966, when the Bronx Borough President Herman Badillo first publicly called for the Center, to mid-1975 when it was first opened for use.

POLICE ATHLETIC LEAGUE-PATROLMAN ANDREW F. GIANNONE-WEBSTER COMMUNITY CENTER, Bronx, New York. Owner: *New York State Urban Development Corporation.* Architects: *Smotrich and Platt Architects.* Engineers: *Robert Silman Associates* (structural); *Arthur L. Zigas & Associates* (mechanical). Graphic designers: *Stuart Handelman and Smotrich and Platt Architects.* Contractor: *E.W. Howell Co., Inc.*

Pilot Center–filling in Over-the-Rhine

Infill, mixed use and neighborhood
context are familiar buzz words in
the professional designer's theoretical
vocabulary. Here, in the Pilot
Center for Cincinnati's Over-the-
Rhine district, designed by
Woollen Associates of Indianapolis,
is an admirable example
of these concepts being put to good
use. The center is a complex of four
separate recreational and social-
service facilities that occupy
what was originally two city blocks,
weaving their way in among older
neighborhood buildings and, on the
street, filling in the gaps while
making semi-enclosed public spaces on
the inside. The new buildings,
by virtue of their scale and materials
and composition, allude, as in the
photograph above, to their older
neighbors even as they assert their own
complexities with painted-on graphics
and with window and door openings.
But their effect is somehow quiet and
modest—they are blessedly unrhetorical
descendants of louder-mouthed
forebearers of the "Yale-Philadelphia,"
or "Inclusivist," design persuasion . . .

"We have been able to add the things people need in order to identify with a community—the social and recreational elements that bring people together," says architect Evans Woollen. "And we have been able to do it with a minimum disruption to the existing fabric." The existing fabric is Cincinnati's Over-the-Rhine district, a neighborhood that is 45 per cent black, 45 per cent Appalachian white, and 10 per cent of German extraction. Over-the-Rhine has been suffering from many of the familiar, self-compounding ills of older urban neighborhoods—deterioration of housing, loss of population, and low average incomes (under $6000 per year) among those who remain. Thus what was once a well-knit social (and architectural) fabric had begun to unravel.

But planners and residents who hoped for a brighter future for Over-the-Rhine did not place their hopes on the *ci-devant* panacea of wholesale urban renewal; instead, they opted for a more meticulous process of retaining whatever old buildings were sound (and therefore retaining the image and character of the district).

Initially, only one part of the district — dubbed the Target Area—was singled out for study by planners, and at its heart was the 1850 Findlay Market, an open-air meat and produce market diagonally across from the A & P store shown in the photograph below. In the planners' view, Findlay Market had an importance to the Target Area analogous to the importance of a shopping center in a contemporary suburb. Most of the key new buildings would be built close by it.

So the Pilot Center is only one cog in the Target Area wheel. It consists of four separate buildings (site plan left) that fill gaps between older buildings and enclose an interior green space. The spire in the photograph on the right is the surviving remnant of an 1840 Roman Catholic church, demolished to make way for a new gymnasium—a loss to the cause of adaptive reuse, and to the architects, who argued for its retention.

New buildings join old ones to form a co-operative partnership

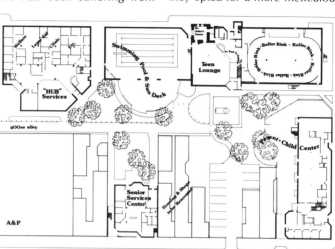

Balthazar Korab photos

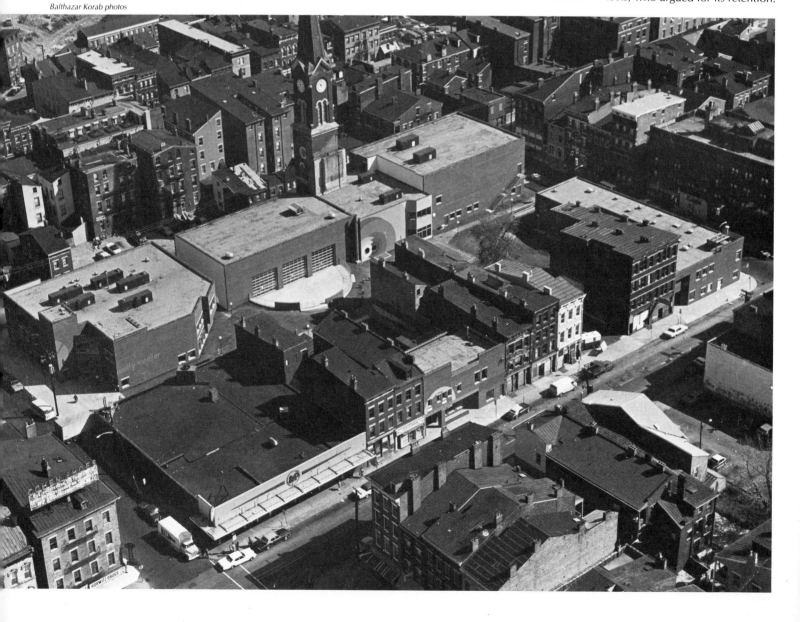

A block-long city street becomes a pedestrian common

In order to maximize contact with local residents, Woollen Associates planned the Pilot Center from a branch office in a store near the site. The largest of four buildings in the Center is the recreational building, seen in part in the photograph below and on the left. It contains a skating rink, games room, crafts room, gym and swimming pool. The pool is in a two-story space enclosed on one side with aluminum and glass

garage doors that can be opened up on warm days to give some sense of connection between the pool and the outdoors. Conversely, two portholes (photo below) give passers'-by the chance to look in at the pool and the swimmers.

Across the pedestrian common from the recreation building is the Senior Citizen Center; it provides low-cost meals, recreational and educational facilities for the elderly. Also across from the rec-

reation building is a Parent-Child facility that houses a Montessori school and a day-care center. The HUB Services building is the heart of Pilot Center; it contains a large community room for local meetings, parties, weddings and movies. In addition, the building provides employee training and placement services, a free store, a small health center and a post office. The architects hoped that this building, like the other ones in

PILOT CENTER

Pilot Center, would provide local residents with a familiar context, rather than a bold and impressive new architectural statement that would run the risk of being forbidding.

The construction cost of Pilot Center was funded by the United States Department of Housing and Urban Development and by the city of Cincinnati whose Department of Urban Development was, with Woollen Associates, also a major contributor to the task of co-ordinating the host of separate organizations that finally made their home in Pilot Center.

PILOT CENTER, Cincinnati, Ohio. Architects: *Woollen Associates—project architects: Laurence O'Connor and David Niland.* Engineers: *Miller, Tallarico McNinch & Hoeffel* (structural); *WHB Associates* (mechanical and electrical). Consultant: *Robert Weinstein* (interiors). General Contractor: *Messer, Perin, Sundahl, Inc.*

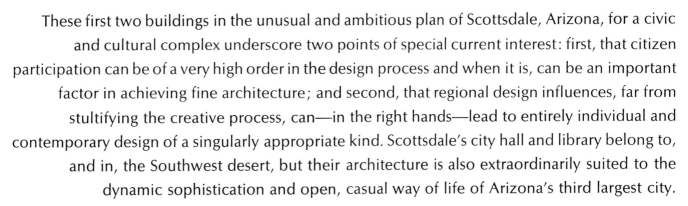

SCOTTSDALE'S
NEW CIVIC CENTER

These first two buildings in the unusual and ambitious plan of Scottsdale, Arizona, for a civic and cultural complex underscore two points of special current interest: first, that citizen participation can be of a very high order in the design process and when it is, can be an important factor in achieving fine architecture; and second, that regional design influences, far from stultifying the creative process, can—in the right hands—lead to entirely individual and contemporary design of a singularly appropriate kind. Scottsdale's city hall and library belong to, and in, the Southwest desert, but their architecture is also extraordinarily suited to the dynamic sophistication and open, casual way of life of Arizona's third largest city.

A CITY HALL THAT INVITES CITIZENS TO PARTICIPATE

The city hall is a building without interior partitions: everything and every process is open and accessible to the public. This is in keeping with the community's conviction that citizens should participate in the processes of their government and that the building which houses these processes should make it easy to do so. A remarkable procedure—the Scottsdale Town Enrichment Program (STEP)—involved some 400 residents, representing every section of the city, in providing direction for planning the center, and the buildings are, says Bennie Gonzales, the architect, a direct translation of STEP's beliefs. The heart of the concept is the use of the central lobby in each building as a community focus. In the city hall, the Council chamber occupies this space; in the library, the periodical lounge. In both buildings the space is sunk four feet below entrance level, with a low balustrade (for leaning by onlookers and overflow audience) surrounding it, and skylighting above through faceted colored glass. Departments to which the public needs ready access are on the main floor. Structure is load-bearing masonry, mortar washed. Slabs and roof beams are of prestressed concrete. Mechanical and electrical lines run in outer walls and in massive interior columns.

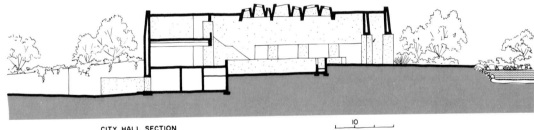

CITY HALL SECTION   10

CITY HALL   N   20

The center is located in what had become a semi-blighted section of town, thanks to a meteoric rise in population—from 12,000 to nearly 70,000—over the previous 10 years. The new buildings and the park in which they are situated have revitalized the area, stimulating private as well as public development. Ultimately the master plan called for developing the remainder of the 20-acre site assembled by the city, to provide facilities for such cultural activities as arts and crafts (an important part of Scottsdale), drama and music.

Similar in plan to the city hall, the library is equally open and inviting, reflecting the informal Southwestern way of life which the Council, in its brief charge to the architects, indicated was one of its criteria for the buildings' design. The central sunken space is used as a periodical lounge, with reading rooms and book shelves in the various reading rooms on the level above. The great central area has the dignity of monumental space but because of the angled direction of the massive columns, is also quite informal. All public services, as well as cataloging and processing, are located on the entrance level. Here, too, is a 100-seat auditorium, accessible from outside the building and from the lobby. On the mezzanine are administrative offices, staff lounge and board room, and a gallery currently used for art exhibitions but ready for expansion. The building was designed for a projected capacity of 125,000 volumes. The furnishings were selected by the architects and are not typical library furniture; some equipment was specially designed.

SCOTTSDALE CIVIC CENTER, Scottsdale, Arizona. Architects: *Gonzales Associates*. Engineers: *Foltz, Hamlyn & Adam, Inc.* (structural); *Richard E. Joachim & Associates* (mechanical); *William E. Meier & Associates* (electrical). Landscape architects: *Gonzales Associates*. General contractor: *Arnold Construction Company*.

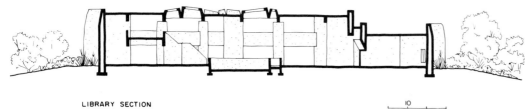

LIBRARY SECTION   10

Similarity in the exterior appearance of the city hall (next page) and the library (shown on this page and the next) is balanced by the strong individuality of each building and influenced by their very different requirements. In the development of the 20-acre civic-cultural center site, the library is a pivotal point.

LIBRARY   N   20

GOOD DECISIONS
AND GOOD DESIGN
PROVIDE A SMALL TOWN
WITH A DISTINGUISHED
CIVIC CENTER

Joshua Freiwald photos

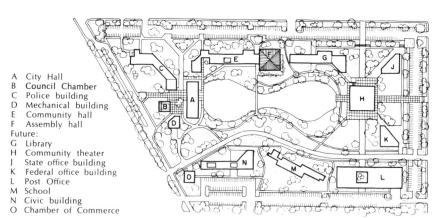

A   City Hall
B   Council Chamber
C   Police building
D   Mechanical building
E   Community hall
F   Assembly hall
Future:
G   Library
H   Community theater
J   State office building
K   Federal office building
L   Post Office
M   School
N   Civic building
O   Chamber of Commerce

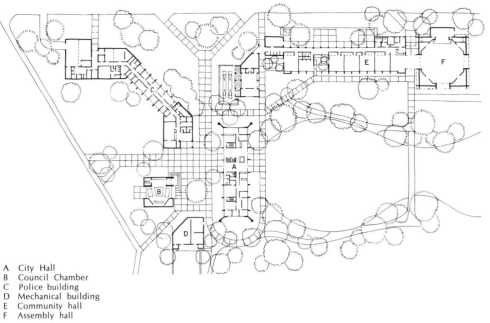

A City Hall
B Council Chamber
C Police building
D Mechanical building
E Community hall
F Assembly hall

Few small towns have the good fortune to have so handsome a civic center as the little northern California town of Fairfield near Travis Air Force Base—or the good sense to make the far-sighted decisions that lead to such a result. It was good fortune, in 1953, that made available to Fairfield a 33-acre tract of land just north of its business section, used during World War II for temporary housing. But it was good sense that the City Council decided to buy it and to keep it intact for eventual use as a civic center. For many years the city worked toward this goal. Finally, emulating three nearby communities whose fine new civic centers had resulted from competitions, Fairfield decided to hold an architectural competition, invited all registered architects in northern and central California to participate, and appointed Louis DeMonte, architect for the Berkeley campus of the University of California, professional advisor. A jury of five professionals chose the design of Robert Wayne Hawley of San Francisco as the winner. His master plan grouped the proposed buildings around a man-made lake (whose jet fountains very practically serve the cooling system) in a parklike setting. The first-phase buildings are now completed: four-story city hall, separate council chamber (a strong statement that the people make the decisions), police administration building (with no jail), community activities building, and 750-seat assembly hall. The same materials—warm red brick and concrete—are used throughout (except for the copper roof on the assembly hall), a limited palette handled with rare versatility and grace to produce an overall design of great distinction.

FAIRFIELD CIVIC CENTER, Fairfield, California. Architects: *Robert Wayne Hawley & Associates*. Engineers: *GFDS Engineers*, structural; *Harding, Miller, Lawson & Associates*, foundation; *Yanow and Bauer*, mechanical/electrical. Consultants: *Wilson, Ihrig & Associates*, acoustical; *Len Koch Co.*, cost. Landscape architects: *Ribera & Sue*. Contractor: *Stolte Inc.*

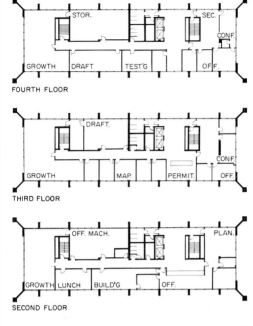

FOURTH FLOOR

THIRD FLOOR

SECOND FLOOR

FIRST FLOOR

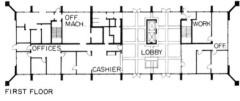

A lively variety among building exteriors gives each its own expression but clearly states that it is one part of a whole design. The city allocated monies for art works to be used in the buildings. The architect advised on selection of 35 prints and 40 commissioned photographs of the area by Ernest Braun. The city bought 40 paintings as prizes in a city-sponsored exhibition.

**A multi-purpose
performing arts center,
part of a mixed-use complex,
attached to a landmark
courthouse
in downtown Syracuse,
New York**

The Onondaga County Civic Center is the first facility to be built on the North American continent that combines government offices and performing arts facilities under one roof, thus in effect providing ongoing financial support for the arts. While this was done as an economy measure, the performing arts facilities have not been subsumed and thereby hidden within the over-all office structure—which might have been even more economical. In this respect, the mixed-use complex in upstate New York is unlike the handful of speculative office buildings constructed in New York City in the past decade which incorporate theaters in return for the zoning incentive of additional floors of rental space. In the latter, the theater portions are identified from the exterior solely by illumination and graphics.

The theater and office complex in Syracuse is adjacent to and connects underground with a fine Neoclassic courthouse, which overlooks a small statue of Christopher Columbus set in a circular fountain. The architects, D. F. Lebensold and Paul Malo—whose respective firms: McAfee, Malo/Lebensold, Affleck, Nichol were combined in joint venture—did not want their huge project to overwhelm the 19th century courthouse and square. They put the performing arts center rather than the office block adjacent to the square and related it in height, width and length to the courthouse.

A pedestrian promenade (opposite page top right) separates the courthouse from the new building. The public foyer in the performing arts center overlooks the square.

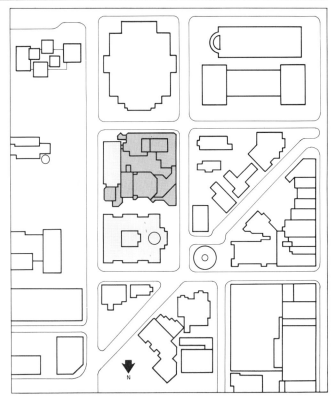

The Civic Center is a three-part building complex: The original eight-story county office building on the site, the new sixteen-story county office building and the performing arts spaces. The latter consists of three theaters: a 2,117-seat concert theater, with two balconies and a proscenium stage; a 480-seat studio theater for experimental productions; and a 300-seat community/rehearsal theater. Collectively, these spaces and the public foyers have been designed to serve as gathering places for the many social, educational, business and political affairs in the community as well as for the performing arts.

Joseph W. Molitor photos

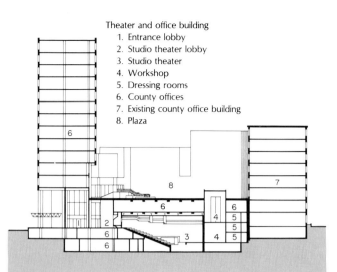

Theater and office building

1. Entrance lobby
2. Studio theater lobby
3. Studio theater
4. Workshop
5. Dressing rooms
6. County offices
7. Existing county office building
8. Plaza

SECTION THROUGH STUDIO THEATER AND OFFICE BUILDING

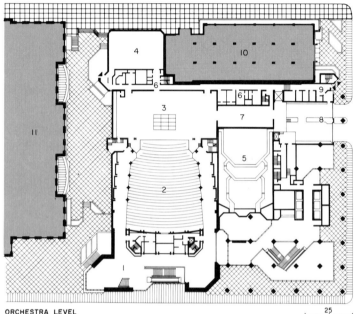

ORCHESTRA LEVEL

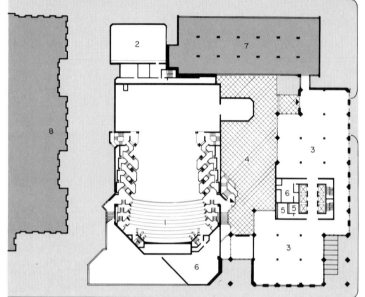

BALCONY LEVEL

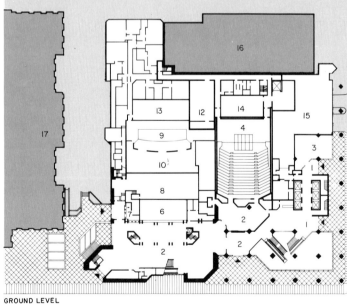

GROUND LEVEL

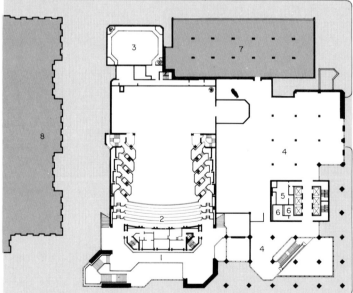

MEZZANINE LEVEL

Ground floor

1. Office lobby
2. Lobby
3. Shop
4. Studio theater
5. Toilet
6. Coat room
7. Box office
8. Administrative offices
9. Orchestra pit
10. Chair storage
11. Dressing rooms
12. Rehearsal room
13. Trap room
14. Workshop
15. Storage
16. Existing county office building
17. Existing county court house

Orchestra level

1. Lobby
2. Orchestra level concert theater
3. Stage
4. Community room
5. Upper part of studio theater
6. Dressing rooms
7. Workshop
8. Truck dock
9. Offices
10. Existing county office building
11. Existing county court house

Mezzanine level

1. Lobby
2. Mezzanine level concert theater
3. Upper part of community room
4. County offices
5. Mechanical
6. Toilet
7. Existing county office building
8. Existing county court house

Balcony level

1. Balcony level concert theater
2. Upper part of community room
3. County offices
4. Outdoor plaza
5. Toilet
6. Mechanical
7. Existing county office building
8. Existing county court house

The principal entrance to the performing arts center (below) leads to the three-story foyer (opposite page top). The entrance to the county office building opens into its own dramatic foyer (above). The public circulation spaces of both the performing arts center and the county office building are particularly grand—an impressive architectural achievement on a site so small in relation to the program that it had to be almost completely covered except for the outdoor promenade. The structure is poured-in-place concrete with walls of brick veneer. The concrete is exposed for the most part on the interior of the performing arts facility with some surfaces of brick or dark oak.

ONONDAGA COUNTY CIVIC CENTER, Onondaga County, Syracuse, New York. Owner: *Onondaga County.* Architects: *McAfee, Malo/Lebensold, Affleck, Nichol (joint venture)—partner-in-charge of design: D. F. Lebensold; second-in-charge of design and administration: Paul Malo; project architect: Isaac Franco; partner-in-charge of administration: Arthur B. Nichol; lighting design: Imre Reichmann.* Consultants: *Montreal-Nicolet, Dressel, Mercille Ltd., Syracuse-Snyder Burns & Associates (structural); Montreal-Langlois, Crossey, Bertrand, Inc., Syracuse-Robson & Woese, Inc. (mechanical/electrical); Russell Johnson Associates (acoustical); Vincent Piacentini (orchestra shell design); Jacques Guillon/Designers Inc. (graphics); Hanscomb, Roy Associates (preliminary costs); Turner Construction (construction costs); Robert Brannigan Associates (theater consultant); William Duffy Inc. (office planning).* Construction management: *Pahl-Turner (joint venture).* Contractor: *E. L. Nezelek, Inc.*

INDEX